Ayana,

Thanks for your support. Wishing you growth + prosperity in all your endeavors!

Ryan

Money *Does* Grow on Trees

Using Collective Economics to
Prove Your Parents Wrong

Money *Does* Grow on Trees

Using Collective Economics to
Prove Your Parents Wrong

GrassRoots Investment Group

GrassRoots Financial Services

For more information, please contact:
info@grig.com

Book design by:
Arbor Books, Inc.
www.arborbooks.com

Printed in the United States of America

Money Does Grow on Trees:
Using Collective Economics to Prove Your Parents Wrong
GrassRoots Investment Group

1. Title 2. Author 3. Business/Success

Library of Congress Control Number: 2007932420

ISBN 10: 0-9798103-0-2
ISBN 13: 978-0-9798103-0-5

Table of Contents

Preface

At the age of 19, an idea was born within me: could a group of individuals learn together, grow together and prosper together? Could the dream of having millions of dollars to invest become a reality someday? Could you grow your own money tree? Have we been taught wrong all these years? Students at Florida A&M University—from Philadelphia, Chicago, Atlanta and Miami—founded GrassRoots Investment Group. Many more joined, and over the years members worked tirelessly to make GrassRoots what it has become today; a nationally recognized organization. What started as a $100-a-month venture has grown to over 40 members from around the world, with over $5 million in assets and generating profit for members every day. This is our story as told by GrassRoots' members—Phillipe Tatem, Marck Dorvil, Vianka Perez Belyea, Harvey Smith and Ryan Williams.

Introduction

Narrated by Phillipe Tatem, GrassRoots Investment Group Founder

I am asked questions all the time, such as: how did you do it? How did you get people to fork over their hard-earned dollars and make such a sacrifice? And what exactly is in it for you?

There was no magic, no hidden agenda, and we didn't come from privileged backgrounds. Instead, as with all great ventures, it all began with a dream.

Unfortunately, dreamers are frowned upon and discouraged in society. I always recall an incident that made a great impact on me when I was a small child. After a major math test, I was daydreaming about becoming a great engineer and was abruptly brought back to reality by my sixth grade teacher screaming at me. My teacher told me to my face, "Phillipe, you will never amount to anything. Stop dreaming!"

Back then, I could never have dreamt of having millions of dollars to invest. However, as luck would have it, at the age of

19, as a second-year undergraduate, I had an idea that evolved into a bold and powerful vision.

It all started with a question: could a group of individuals learn together, grow together and prosper together? Could it be something so simple that anyone could do it? Does money really grow on trees?! Were my parents wrong all these years?!

My parents always told me that life was difficult and that money didn't grow on trees. I used to dream about going into the backyard and picking a few dollars off the oak tree, to buy my grandma something special when she visited at our house. Money didn't come easily growing up, but I knew that one day, I would get my money tree.

I now know the answer to those questions, but in the humble beginnings of GrassRoots Investment Group, nothing was guaranteed.

We were just students at Florida A&M when we founded GrassRoots Investment Group, affectionately known by its acronym: GRIG. Our mission remains simple: to create generational wealth through sustained returns on investments and promote mindshare through education and networking. And with the marking of the tenth anniversary of GRIG, we are now a renowned, nationally recognized investment organization.

So let us share our unique story with you in the hope that others will not only replicate our success, but also learn from our mistakes. There have definitely been a few!

When I look back on how this investment group got started, it brings bittersweet memories. It was the summer of

1997 and I was engrossed in my corporate internship at a major bank in New York City. It was my first time in New York and it was very different from anything I had ever experienced. At that time of year, the air tasted of hot asphalt, yet inside, the air conditioner was pumped up high. I could practically see the suits getting chills as they walked inside the building.

For a while, it seemed like my life was full of promise. Everything I wanted was right there, inside the walls of a New York bank. I was so excited! In fact, I could think of nothing but becoming a big-time corporate banker. I could smell the green money seeping from the vault and mingling with the cool air. What could be more thrilling?

However, before long, I was hit with the harsh reality of corporate politics. I realized that big business was not interested in fair play, and that it would take more than a job to make my dreams a reality. The idea of inclusion and diversity was still an academic ideal, but merely a foreign concept to management at the bank. As a minority in a majority-dominated environment, this was truly a wake-up call for me. I had joined an exclusive club of "gentlemen" who took every opportunity to let me know that my input and presence were not welcomed.

Although I didn't know it at the time, my experience was invaluable. It opened my mind to the concept that success was not going to come in the form of a diversity program or a changing corporate culture. No, the real winners were always the clients of the bank—those who had created wealth for themselves and who set their own agendas. They planted the seeds to their money trees and watched them grow.

Though I thrived in this environment and produced great results during my internship, it forced me to think about how I could escape such a place. Could I truly find freedom? Can you? I knew that spending those long hours working at the bank wasn't the life for me. I wanted to give myself options other than following the well-trodden footsteps of the previous generation: educate, work, save, retire, die. How boring!

It dawned on me that I was living the life of my parents. They had worked hard for many years to take care of their responsibilities and save for retirement. They taught me this discipline growing up and that—simply put—a good job with benefits signified success. My idea of success was vastly different from theirs.

My parents had always told me that getting an education was key to getting a good job. It is true that excelling in the classroom will result in better chances of landing that high-paying executive lifestyle with perks that many of us salivate over. But then, there is always that one burning question aching in the backs of our minds: Is this all that life has to offer?

Don't get me wrong. I respect my parents and all they have given me. They sacrificed much to raise four children and often worked several jobs to make ends meet. However, I look back and can't help but think that their advice would have had more impact and been more inspiring if they had shown me something—anything—beyond working for the likes of what I experienced in New York, and suffering through it just because it paid well.

I remember reading a quote from sociologist and author W. E. B. Dubois around the same time that I was working at the bank. He said that the most talented among us will help steer the masses. Upon reading this, it struck me that it was my obligation, as one of those talented individuals and as a man, to do more than just meet my parents' expectations. I have always defined true freedom as the ability to have choice without consequences.

Don't you think that we need to encourage the dreamers and show them how to empower those dreams? It was with this idea that I decided to form an investment club. Although it might sound strange, it seemed like the perfect choice.

I began to think of ways that my friends—who I thought were some of the most talented and interesting individuals I had met in my short life—and I could free ourselves from taking this deeply entrenched path. Basically, I didn't just want to buck the trend for myself. Instead, I hoped to create an organization that helped others empower themselves, setting an agenda that would perpetually benefit those who followed—an economic rights movement, if you will.

What if we got together, I thought, and pooled our resources? What if we started our own organization with members who learned from and invested with each other? What if we could create something that gave members the choice to work or not? These thoughts overwhelmed me, and I knew then that our plan was destined for success.

It was not an easy task, but it was well worth it. And I think the members (and my friends) of GRIG would agree. This story is told through the voices of the following members, all of who came to GRIG at various points and in different ways: me; Phillipe Tatem, one of the founding members;

Harvey Smith, one of the original members; Ryan Williams, a ten-year member; Marck Dorvil, a seven-year member; and Vianka Perez Belyea, a member who joined the group after reading the first national magazine article on GRIG.

Just as I proposed the following ideas to them...I propose the same to you!

Chapter 1
Don't Be Afraid

Narrated by Phillipe Tatem

"Imagination is more important than knowledge."

I had been reading about investment clubs during the year prior to starting my banking internship. One thing that college taught me was that the entrepreneurial spirit and the disciplined approach of investing was a way—possibly the only way—for a person like me to radically transform the game.

Things fell into place one sunny morning during my internship. A fellow intern was reassigned to alphabetize files in a dark, stuffy closet. At best the place could be described as a cave; at worst, a prison. And I instantly saw it. I knew I wasn't actually alone and that there were, in actuality, many smart, talented and driven individuals who were probably thinking the same thing I was: *I've gotta get out of here.*

It reinforced my view that things had to change and that by combining forces with others I could not only reduce my risks and increase my chances of success, but create an opportunity for others. I became energized and began recruiting. Needless to say, my fellow intern, Charles Frazier, who was all but entombed in that dark and awful closet and whose grunts and moans requesting a standard cubicle with a lamp were often heard reverberating from the elevator, was one of GRIG's first members.

Charles and I were both seeking our MBAs from the School of Business and Industry at Florida A&M University, and we often conversed about networking as a means of achieving economic empowerment. We discussed on occasion how the vast majority of people seemed to lack investment savvy. Also, we spent time researching investment groups as a way to learn, educate and help build a financial legacy that could be used to provide for our futures, without having to rely on a potentially insolvent Social Security fund. These conversations resonated with me. Now was the time to invest and create our future financial independence, and hopefully create a generational legacy for our kids and grandkids.

It was not easy to convince people that they were never too young (or too old) to begin investing. The biggest initial challenge for a fledgling organization called GrassRoots Investment Club was finding more members—the "roots" that would grow into a powerful force—who were willing to hand over their money to turn a dream into a reality.

There Is No Gain Without Sacrifice
The average investment club's dues were about $25 per month—not small change for a group of college students who,

at best, had part-time jobs in pizza parlors. Some were fortunate enough to have found paid summer internships, too. But still, as any graduate can attest, every penny counts when living on campus.

However, I really wanted to up the ante. This wasn't going to be your average investment club. The term "club" just didn't seem to sum up the ideals we were working toward. Our goal was to make serious money, which meant that sacrifice would be the key to our eventual success. Thus, the name GrassRoots Investment Club was changed to GrassRoots Investment Group.

The dues were set at $100 per month and we expected long-term commitments from our members. I knew this was going to be hard on my peers. But the members who joined recognized that it would take commitment to really see this through. Another aspect was setting a 30-year initial charter to communicate that this was not going to be a short-lived, get-rich-quick scheme. This was real.

From my research during those planning stages, most investment clubs seemed socially motivated, like mixers where members casually invested in stocks for education and minor profit. Obviously, if we were going to truly leverage our organization to replace corporate employment and provide real wealth for our members, it would require less "social" investing and a deeper commitment. There would have to be sacrifices in order to stay focused and buck the traditional thoughts of educate, work, save, retire, die!

The first year of GRIG saw a strengthening of relationships and the resolve of commitment among members. For some, the $100-a-month dues had already proven to be troublesome. In fact, it was a running joke that one member had her electricity cut off, yet paid her GRIG dues on time. Her hair told the whole story as she entered meetings looking like she'd been out in a hurricane.

Aside from a few nights sitting in the dark, this was a small sampling of the focus we required from our members. It was this kind of dedication and strength of character that would propel the group into the big leagues.

Looking back, the people who I asked to join were opinionated, passionate and determined to prove their points, yet all were from different backgrounds. It became clear that the GRIG organization had been formed based on diversity in thought, skill set and expertise. Obviously, this could have been a dangerous recipe, which might have led to infighting and the butting of heads. Naturally, this led to differences of opinion, but in the end, we came together to move the group forward.

The First Meeting
I pulled up a chair and took a deep breath as I gazed around the room at the first members. I was feeling energized and couldn't believe that a summer spent organizing members was finally resulting in the first face-to-face meeting. This was an exciting day for all of us! We were wired and buzzing around the room like a bunch of bees in a hive.

Since the idea of an investment group was introduced over the phone, this was literally the first time some members had laid eyes on one another. My heart began to beat faster and faster as I kicked off the first meeting. We were about to grow that money tree.

Selecting officers is an important part of establishing any organization and therefore, it was the number one item we needed to address. The officers had to be credible, inspiring and aligned with the overall vision of the group. As they would essentially be dealing with our members' money, it was vital that everyone feel confident with the people who were collecting and managing GRIG's funds.

I took it upon myself to pick the first team to lead GRIG. I knew, even then, that the early stages of an organization are when it is most vulnerable. Just one mistake, one slip-up— however minor—could end the group forever. I wanted it to be simple and straightforward, with five leadership positions: senior partner, junior partner, financial partner, recording partner and the parliamentarian. These positions are defined below:

Senior Partner
Responsible for setting strategic vision
Coordinate and preside over meetings
Oversee company activities
Official group representative

Junior Partner
Ensure execution of strategic vision
Assumption of Senior Partner duties in their absence
Ensure operational efficiencies within the group

Financial Partner
Collect and distribute funds
Maintain books about financial operations, assets, and member shares
Issue receipts to partners and members
Compile financial reports

Recording Partner
Keep record of company activities
Maintain group roster and key information
File and maintain legal documents
Report on previous meetings

Parliamentarian
Interpret operating agreement
Update operating agreement as necessary
Maintain meeting order according to Roberts Rules of Order
Tie-breaker for Management team

Fortunately, I already had an idea of who should be part of the team, as I needed to pick people who had credibility with the other members. My roommate became the senior partner, while I took the financial partner position. The junior and recording partner positions were filled with credible members. The parliamentarian position was left unfilled, but I had the perfect person in mind.

The use of these titles actually had significance; the group was not going to have presidents and vice presidents. This would have been too formal, especially as the goal was mutual ownership and participation. The positions were created for partners to serve, facilitate and handle leadership duties, though, in essence, it was everyone's responsibility to be leaders of our group. In addition, each position has a term of two years to allow members the opportunity to participate in a management capacity. As with any organization, people are its most important asset. As I often said, the passion, commitment and energy of leadership cannot be substituted.

Getting the Rules Down

Although setting our rules of operations was done before the first meeting, it has evolved as the organization has grown. It is very important to get a clear set of rules that all members agree to follow. There are many samples online, but the National Association of Investors Corporation (www. better-investing. org) is a great place to start. You can also visit grig. com and view our first operating agreement. Every game has a set of rules and investing is no different. When it comes to allocating profit, collecting dues, electing officers, legal protections and even running monthly meetings, it must be clear to get successful results.

You should also remember that rules will never cover everything and if there is one thing that is important, *when rules fail, values prevail.* The members in the organization must be aligned to the mission and goals. This will help fill in gaps as you grow.

Creating a Culture

Now that the leadership team and rules were created, the next big thing was jelling as an organization. We began to talk to each other about our goals and fears as we approached graduation. We learned that we shared similar objectives, and discussed how we could begin to help each other reach our goals. Someone was smiling on us, because we definitely connected.

While the monetary value of the group was increasing, the organization began to act very much like a family. Being a GRIG member meant something more than making money. It was a rite of passage, a validation that working together to win was more than just words. But most of all, it was a refreshing escape from our everyday lives. We shared a common interest, and leveraging each other's skills seemed to be paying off in a big way. We were creating a "burning platform"—a crisis, engineered to force change—that would have a transformational effect on the individuals involved, and potentially have a greater impact on society at large.

We had been taught that the individual was king and that working hard and educating yourself was the sure path to getting ahead. We didn't realize that our investment group was going to buck that trend. As we began to talk and explore our interests, we learned that we didn't need money or ideas to get ahead.

Could this be real?

Could working together really change the game?

The first two years of the organization were dedicated to joint growth and creating a culture. We were also developing a strong reputation for success. The tag line of the organization began to reverberate with members and external parties: "Prosperity Runs Deep in the Roots."

The ideas of prosperity, mutual sacrifice and family seemed so counterintuitive to making money with a bunch of strangers, as is the case with most investment clubs. The organization leveraged the characteristics of our members and used their knowledge to turn GRIG into a blossoming business. Before we really knew it ourselves, we had become everything we aimed to be—namely, an organization of professional and business-minded individuals whose primary goal was to secure financial freedom over time.

We began to answer the kind of questions that are posed in insurance commercials: what if life deals you a blow—unemployment, bankruptcy, injury? Are your individual successes sustainable? Will you be able to recover and overcome? Where would you seek support and safe harbor? Could it be GRIG?

Lessons can be learned by looking all around us. One that resonates with our organization is the fable "Lessons from the Geese":

In the fall, when you see geese heading south for the winter, flying along in a "V" formation, you might be interested in knowing what science has discovered about why they fly that way.

It has been learned that as each bird flaps its wings, it creates uplift for the bird immediately following. By flying in "V" formation, the whole flock adds at least a 71 percent greater flying range than if each bird flew on its own. Quite similar to people who are working as part of a team and share a common direction, they get where they are going quicker and easier because they are traveling on the trust of one another and lifting each other up along the way. Whenever a goose falls out of formation, it suddenly feels the drag and resistance of trying to go through it alone and quickly gets back into formation, to take advantage of the power of the flock.

If we have as much sense as these clever geese, we will stay in formation and share information with those who are headed in the same way that we are going. Furthermore, when the lead goose gets tired, he rotates back in the wings, and another goose takes over. This could tell us that it really does pay to share leadership and take turns doing hard jobs.

Also, the geese honk from behind to encourage those up front to maintain their speed. Words of support and inspiration help energize those on the front line, helping them to keep pace in spite of day-to-day pressures and fatigue. So, it is important that our honking be encouraging. Otherwise it's just…well, honking!

Finally, it's interesting to note that when a goose gets sick, or is wounded and falls out, two geese follow the injured one down to help and protect him. They stay with him until he is either able to fly or dead, and then they launch again with another formation to catch up with their group.

Thus, when one of us is down, it's up to the others to stand by and support us in our time of trouble. If we follow these lessons from the geese, we will stand by each other when things get rough. We will stay in formation with those headed where we want to go. So the next time you see a formation of geese, remember their message: it is indeed a reward, a challenge and a privilege to be a contributing member of a team.

This model, based on certain migration characteristics of geese, has been applied to the concepts of human behavior and teamwork at many a management seminar. And, similarly, it has been replicated across GRIG as members help each other with jobs, financial advice and everyday life challenges, allowing us to sustain ourselves over the past decade.

Individually, I'm not sure we would have survived, but together, we grew. There is power in numbers and collective focus! We've learned the fundamental truths that the group is smarter than its smartest person, and that the sum is greater than its individual parts. The collective group of GRIG has been able to continuously step up to the plate and overcome. There is power in numbers and we need each other to help us along in this challenging journey. We owe it to previous generations that sacrificed everything, in wars and human indignity, to rise above the spirit of self and make an impact on this world.

I started this organization to secure financial independence for myself and everyone involved. I wanted to prove once and for all that the money tree does exist if you want it. I also wanted to give people something my generation didn't have: the precious choice not to work. This is why we've created an organization that feels like a family but acts like a business. We're not only an investment group that contributes regularly to build financial wealth; we take a genuine interest in the well being of our culture and each individual who is a part of our family.

Mostly, we all believe in the powerful concept of collective economics and realize that united we stand, divided we fall— which is why it would be a disgrace if we didn't share our story and inspire others to do the same.

Ask yourself this: why go into something alone? Together, you can be stronger, smarter and have less risk of failure and loss. Starting an investment group might not be an easy task, but with passion and dedication anything is achievable. The real secret to success is the understanding that you can't achieve it alone. The faster you realize that your network and surroundings impact your ability to make things happen, the sooner you will be on the road to riches. The investment group approach is a proven method to functionally make it work.

What I Learned

• Don't be afraid to dream.

• Understand the importance of your personal network.

• When choosing charter members, look for individuals who share the vision. This will drive sustainability and consistency of membership.

• Dues set the tone of the organization. Setting them too low could mean the difference between a casual group and something more serious.

• An investment group requires sacrifice to get it right. It is important to make that point at your initial meeting.

Chapter 2
Establishing the Structure
Narrated by Harvey Smith

"Soon our blood pressure would be sizzling, just like the pancake batter."

I remember when I was first introduced to the idea of GRIG. It still surprises me that I was even recruited as one of the original members, especially since I personally knew only one of the core charter members, Phillipe, and only then in a limited context. So I treated my recruitment to join as a peer in this new venture as something special. I never knew what kind of impact I would have on GRIG...or what impact it would have on me.

I always wanted to place my mark on something big, but my personality and background didn't seem to be leading me into that direction. In school, one of the major lessons constantly taught by our professors was the power of our network. It's a lesson that will stay with me for the rest of my life. But when you're an out-of-state student without a scholarship, you tend to focus on the things that keep you in school. In order, my priorities were my campus job, my studies and then what I thought were extracurricular activities: fun and developing my network.

But by the time I ended my second year in school, I knew something was missing. I wasn't participating in campus activities because I was so committed to my job. For that matter, I was barely participating in my studies. I started out strong in my first year but had disappointing performance in my second year. So, in the fall of 1997—the beginning of my junior year—I knew I needed to do something different. I just didn't know what that would be. Fortunately, Phillipe was one of the first people I ran into, and little did I know that he had a plan for me.

The Man With the Plan
Phillipe and I met my freshman year. A sophomore at the time, he was in my fundamentals of engineering class. We were both at the business school, but were required to take some engineering classes to round out our knowledge bases.

The instructor was extremely boring and Phillipe and I both would exchange a few words in the back of the class just to keep awake. In some cases, a few jokes would help keep us from missing the intricacies of the topic of the day. We eventually finished the semester, but continued to share a nod or two across campus when we saw each other. So, when he stopped me in the hall to set up a meeting with him, I had a glimmer of hope that this year would be much different than the last.

At the time, I didn't personally know Phillipe. He was known around campus as a respected leader in the Student Government Association (SGA) and within the business school. Not being involved with campus politics or being a leader within the business school, I wondered why he wanted to meet with me. We shared one class, but that was all.

I agreed, and a few days later, I met him in one of the halls at the business school. He asked me if I would like to join an investment group that he had just formed. Phillipe mentioned he thought I was a motivated person who would fit right in with the others in the group. All the jokes and conversation in the back of class had actually been my first informal interview.

Phillipe also mentioned how this would be good for my personal development, as I could enhance my network within school, which would make my graduate years much easier. He didn't have to sell too much before I knew I was highly interested. A few weeks later, I found myself driving up to an apartment complex, where the parking lot was packed with cars, to attend my first meeting.

Meeting the Group

The lot was dark and all the apartments looked the same. Some of the apartment numbers were missing, and I couldn't help but wonder what type of place this was! I ended up knocking on the wrong door, interrupting some poor student's studies. After having the door angrily slammed in my face, I got my bearings and finally found the right apartment.

Gaining my composure, I rang the bell and a girl answered the door. She looked a little scary as she ushered me inside. As I walked down the hall, I saw what seemed to be about 30 people in a living room, stuffed onto the couch, sitting on the stairs, standing along the walls and perched in front of a table. All eyes were on me. I heard some whispers: "Who's the new guy?" "Do you know him?" "Doesn't he look familiar?" "He's kinda cute." Well, I *thought* I heard someone call me cute.

The intimidating figure who answered the door then came up to me. Her name was Nkenge Harmon and she was a close friend of Phillipe and a member of the organization. She gave me a hug, which was quickly followed by one from Phillipe. She wasn't that scary after all; I guess the light that was behind her made her look a little unapproachable as she answered the door. Soon, I was asked to introduce myself to everyone. In turn, everyone then introduced themselves to me.

Harvey, the Parliamentarian

The senior partner at the time explained to me that although this was the second meeting, I really only missed the initial selection of the leadership. He also mentioned that some of the people standing around hadn't yet committed to the group. They wound up asking me why I wanted to join the group and what I felt I could provide to the organization.

I don't remember how I answered. I think I was a little embarrassed because I was younger than everyone else and didn't really know anyone there. I guess my response was good enough, though, because they voted me in on the spot.

Their faith in me became more apparent when Phillipe made a motion to appoint me as the parliamentarian of the group, which was unanimously accepted. Little did I know they had already targeted me as the first person to fill this position.

At the time, I didn't even know what a parliamentarian was, let alone what one did. But I took on the challenge because I knew that no matter what happened next, it would help me grow as an individual.

This was my whirlwind introduction to the family that had only been known for the past month as the GrassRoots Investment Group.

Down to Business

With the formalities of being appointed parliamentarian out of the way, I soon found myself thrust right into the middle of the action in the group. The first thing I had to do was moderate the monthly meetings and facilitate our diverse membership's agreeing to a course of action. This seemed like *Mission: Impossible*, since the most active members were all part of the school's Student Government Association where they were senators. The implication was that these few members had deft abilities to debate issues and carry conversations. The less assertive members, especially those who felt like they were novice investors, wouldn't even attempt to join into the discussions. This was especially true in situations where there was ambiguity surrounding the written rules.

These written rules are referred to as an "operating agreement," which can be thought of as the constitution of an organization. This type of document is also sometimes referred to as "by-laws." The operating agreement defines the name of the organization and its mission, how people join and leave and what they're expected and obligated to do while members. It encompasses the most basic, unchanging tenets of the people it represents.

This was the main resource I used to help ensure that the more assertive members did not just have their way with the group. One thing that I thought about during these conversations was that no matter how talented or versed in debate any of them were, everyone would equally benefit from the actions of the group.

Nkenge was definitely one of the more assertive members. Headstrong and smart, her personality and presence helped to temper the testosterone of the many males that then comprised the group. She would let you know that she was the most dedicated member of the group and willing to miss a meal in order to pay her dues. She was one of the partners who took an immediate interest in me, just because of the testimony and experience Phillipe had with me.

Nkenge's openness also played a pivotal role in the development of our first recruited partner, Wendell Holden. Wendell joined the group a few months after we started; he knew Phillipe and Nkenge because they served in SGA together. In the beginning, Wendell was quite reserved. But at the encouragement of Phillipe and Nkenge, he quickly asserted himself and developed a personality that would impact GRIG time and again.

I immediately had to strike a delicate balance between these assertive members, while at the same time encouraging dissenting viewpoints and keeping the conversation constructive. Initially, debate centered on pending investments and the differing strategies we would employ on behalf of the group. But we also had heated discussions on admitting people outside of our core business school network. This was something that took time and maturity to overcome.

GRIG's Initial Investment Strategy

Despite this, the first couple months as parliamentarian were relatively easy for me. First, I focused on learning about the different people in the group. Also, we didn't invest for the first few months so that we could build up cash to fund our first investment.

As a result, the meetings were very social: we would always have cake, and we spent the first 20 minutes or so just catching up and talking about school. People would be late to the meetings and we would often make small talk as we waited for them.

Once we officially started a meeting, we would go through the agenda. The meetings were loose. People would crack jokes and talk in private circles if the agenda items got too boring. This was also the time when we had our fledgling educational sessions.

Although I didn't know it at the time, I later discovered that this all foreshadowed exactly how our group would invest. The combination of our youth, the enthusiasm about mastering our own financial destinies and working with the people we regarded as our social leaders guided our group into equally compelling investment philosophies, with little regard to any fundamental or sound investment strategy.

As soon as we were ready to begin investing, we started to see more excitement in our organization. For example, two months before we were to start investing, we came up with a stock selection sheet, where we listed companies that we were going to research. We decided that the easiest way for us to make money and build our money tree was to invest in the stock market.

The selection of our initial companies was made by following the advice given to many new investment clubs: we picked the companies that we often patronized. Two months later, there were motions made to add many more companies to the original sheet, despite a lack of research. Supporters of these additions advocated their positions by saying that the companies originally picked were not going to be as profitable as their "hot stocks," while the detractors defended themselves by saying that at least their picks were researched.

Unfortunately, even the "researched" stocks were shaky, as no one had any fundamental understanding as to what findings should sway an "invest" or "no-invest" decision. Even today, it's hard to get professional advisors to provide a straight answer to that question. Now we know that the answer depends on your individual circumstances, goals, education, investment experience, actions in the economy and the market.

As debate ensued about selecting investments based on principled research or on making quick money, the "family meeting" started to look more like a Wall Street trading pit. What began as the partners' calm dialogue on the merits of an investment selection degraded to yelling. Then, just when we calmed everyone down and decided which stocks we would purchase, someone asked if we should be saving money for a McDonald's franchise! We were already talking like we had a million dollars to invest instead of just $3,000!

The Passion of the GRIG
One bit of knowledge that we lacked at GRIG was how to take the raw emotion out of the process without losing the members' passion and zeal. We had many exciting moments in our meetings. In hindsight, we could've done things a lot more

effectively if we'd had a solid system to channel the extra emotions into something more constructive. Fortunately, this comes with time, and with experience in investing with and relating to people and their money.

Like many new investment clubs, we lived and died by the monthly meeting's tally on the performance of our investments. It was boring to look at the daily fluctuations in our stock's prices and much more exciting to see the people on CNBC talk about investing buzzwords and catchphrases, such as "PE ratio," "gainers leading decliners" and "x stock just reached a new 52-week high." Months seemed like eternities when our stocks weren't going up. But, it *wasn't* that our stocks weren't going up; it was always that other stocks were gaining faster than the ones we picked.

What's More Risky: Investors or Investments?
I remember one stock we picked—Iridium Holdings. It was presented by one of our partners who, arguably, had a decent understanding of investing and the telecommunications industry. Iridium was supposed to be the first company that was going to market mobile phones that could be used anywhere in the world, via a network of 66 satellites. The company research was polished and well presented. The partner extolled the virtues of a growing, technologically capable society that could use satellite phones in the middle of the Atlantic ocean, if desired.

I remember Nkenge playing devil's advocate with this pick. Fervid debate ensued, as many of us thought this would be a good "tech" play that we could take a long-term position on. This was back in 1997 or 1998, when cell phones were more of a luxury and were priced accordingly. At that time, we were too naive to understand that even well-funded companies can lose big.

Iridium wound up declaring bankruptcy even before the last satellite was launched. The reason: service charges began at $7 per minute. Even though there was a market to talk in the middle of the ocean (say, from an oil rig in the Gulf of Mexico), 10 customers talking all day at $7 per minute can't pay for 66 satellites to be in the air to route the expensive calls. Besides, when was the last time the average person paid $7 a minute to talk on the phone?

This is proof that all the passion in the world can't keep satellites in outer space, or a bad investment from heading south. It's also proof that investors, not investments, are the most risky part of investing.

Breaking Up Is Hard to Do

Iridium was only one company among a sea of thousands, all begging us to add them to our portfolio. Before we got really engrossed with every move of the market, we would face our first major challenge.

Nine months after GRIG started, we held our final meeting before the majority of the group left school for the summer. Many of us had internships that took us to places such as New York, Colorado, Mexico, Kenya, and the United Kingdom. Everyone in leadership positions, including Phillipe, our financial partner at that time, would be out of the country.

This would be the first true test of the group. We didn't want to stop investing just because we wouldn't physically be together. Besides, this would provide us with crucial practice and insight as to how we would operate the group when the majority of us graduated within a year and went wherever the winds of Corporate America would take us.

Ultimately, the issue concerned the logistics of how to carry on administratively when all members were decentralized. Some of the practical issues included how we would conduct meetings, who would purchase or sell stock and how we would deposit capital contributions during the hiatus. Was GRIG strong enough to make such a transition? Or would our members lose sight of the group amid the high-paying internships?

Fortunately, the answer was found in the collective passion of the group. We adopted ever more creative attempts to emulate the face-to-face meetings GRIG was founded on. We started by transitioning our business to the Internet. We conducted email updates of group business among the active members. This was supplemented by one-on-one phone calls and physical visits to less active members to obtain their proxy approval of different initiatives. Nkenge and Wendell wound up being instrumental in coordinating our summer activities.

This eventually evolved into our obtaining the GRIG. com domain name and distributing personalized email addresses among members, to foster pride in our brand. We used the Website as a repository, to store meeting minutes and financial reports. After the majority of us graduated, we conducted low-cost teleconferences by getting everyone who had three-way calling on their phones to connect everyone for our monthly meetings. We have plenty of stories of members' cell phones dropping calls and disconnecting half of a meeting's attendees!

Our current system includes meeting monthly via free tele-conferencing services. General and managing partners each have standing meetings on alternating months, with additional meetings on an as-needed basis. We supplement the meetings with tons of email correspondence. Voting takes place via emails to our parliamentarian or sometimes, via voice-vote during the teleconferences. We try to debate issues via email and one-on-one calls, so that general meetings can be reserved for action instead of endless matters that should be resolved prior to our meetings.

The CNBC Boys

As GRIG was nearing the conclusion of its first year, we had a fairly good idea as to who the group's leaders were, in contrast with those who could be considered the "social loafers." Even though Phillipe was not the senior partner, he held the respect of the group. Over the course of the summer, we strategized a new vision for the group. Our work would lay the foundation for what would become the most exciting time in GRIG's short history. The vision would be solidified when Phillipe and I became roommates later that year.

During the summer, many members saw the beginnings of the tech wave. The tech company, Yahoo!, had been trading for a full year and had already split three times. Many companies with "dot com" after their names were rumored to be getting ready for their IPOs—their initial public offerings, or the first sales of the corporations' stocks to the general public.

The stigmatism of dot-com companies was beginning to wane in the financial press as the Yahoo!s of the investing world didn't immediately shrivel up and die, as some prognosticators were predicting. More and more companies were making the switch to online-only business models. The naivety of the market was slowly being outstripped by its greed.

Unfortunately, our group would fall victim to this dot-com mania. Thinking back, the Dow Jones Industrial Average was 8500, which was up about 10 percent from when GRIG was established. The summer was a rollercoaster ride for the market and we felt like things were going to take off again very soon.

When Phillipe and I became roommates that fall, we rented a big-screen TV that was invariably tuned to the CNBC financial news channel. Because of Phillipe's class schedule, he could tune in at the most exciting time of day. As soon as I walked in the door, he would tell me what the new hot stocks were, and got me to help convince the group that we should apply to our broker to buy IPOs and trade on margin (loan backed by stock). It wasn't a tough sell, as it seemed so easy to make money, and all the stocks were going up.

Phillipe and I personally called each member to get the votes we needed to buy the hot stocks. We passed notes in class, discussing what stocks we should buy and who we might lobby for the vote on establishing a strategy so that we could trade stocks on a daily basis.

GRIG Gone Wild

Phillipe and I were very excited and wanted to aggressively move the group toward day trading. Although a few partners did not feel comfortable about it, several events worked in our favor to establish the day trading strategy. All the stars were aligning to make it a very interesting run.

First, our membership was slashed from nearly 20 people to only 12 by the end of the summer. The drop was due to people not being disciplined enough to maintain both $100 monthly dues and their college lifestyles.

Second was the power of the "Chicago vote," which were a block of votes that Phillipe held for his friends from high school—people he personally recruited and who trusted him to vote in their best interest. At its height, Phillipe effectively controlled more than 30 percent of the group's voting power.

Last, the group was looking for creative ways to improve investment results over the summer's poor performance. This, combined with the group's passion, would lay the foundation for GRIG to become accomplished day traders.

Now that we had support for the day trading strategy, we were ready to invest in the latest companies listed on the U. S. stock market. We began analyzing and selecting stocks and created an internal evaluation process. Believe it or not, the first stock the partners purchased proved to be successful. It seemed like the group couldn't lose while using our stock evaluating process. In a matter of months, we were gaining 15 percent on every investment!

Of course, this created even more excitement as companies such as America Online, Apple Computer and Yahoo! were quickly added to the portfolio. The group followed our analysis, but this method was soon replaced by the desire to buy any stock talked about by the financial media. Over time, the stock evaluator became less important and was replaced by members' impassioned pleas to pick up stocks featured on CNBC, simply because they were the "must-buys" of the day.

Now, because of the increase in activity, we found that we were outgrowing our group's operating rules. To correct this unintended shortcoming, we made a major change by adding an automatic buy rule. This rule stated that any stocks we owned that dropped in value by 20 percent or more would be automatically repurchased, and would be sold once they increased back to their original values. This was significant, as it would utilize our margin capacity if necessary and would do so without any additional voting. Speed was instrumental in realizing this aspect of our day trading strategy.

We were on a roll until the market took a slight dip. This caused the partnership to lose confidence, doubt the market and want to pause further investing.

To continue to push our initiative, Phillipe suggested that we talk to all centers of influence to support the day trading strategy. Our key ally turned out to be Nkenge. She had influence over the biggest naysayers of the group—including Wendell, whose favorite word was "sell!" As a result of great disagreement and potential deadlock, Nkenge sent this email to the group:

Brothers and Sisters,

Well, I read the minutes from the last meeting. This might have been the most effective way to encourage my return. What do you mean by "we are waiting for a less volatile market to invest"!? You have money sitting in the bank and you think that [it's a] good idea? Who is watching the market every day and has the divine intuition to say that it is no longer volatile?

Surely, we understand that YOU CANNOT TIME THE MARKET. Sure, let's wait until stocks are more expensive again—then, we'll feel more comfortable about buying them like everybody else. For our information, partners, the market has just gone up six days in a row for the first time in months. Tech stocks [are] also shooting up. Finally, are we afraid now to pay too much for something? We are likely to miss out on the current bargains on stocks that fell irrationally and thus, miss potential gains. (Opportunity cost, anyone?) This, I remind you, is what we had hoped for: a bona fide buying opportunity.

Remember how we sat in the living room last fall as a group, watched CNBC and cheered as the market fell? Here it is again. Why have you stopped cheering? Don't tell me $20,000 is enough to put stars in our eyes. We don't have enough money in the market to be sad about. Yes, I may feel differently in 20 years, when we are closer to our investment horizon. You know, Goldman held up its IPO until the market will receive it better—that is, pay a higher price for it. I guess they think stocks are too cheap right now, too. Let's get the money out of the bank!!!

It wouldn't be long before we got even more money out of the bank and into wildly speculative investments. The best example of this occurred in November 1998. We were approved for the IPO of Earthweb, then a publisher of websites that supported information technology professionals. Phillipe originally motioned for the purchase of 2500 shares at an expected IPO price of $15 to $21 per share. The amount was even more than we had on hand in cash and margin capacity, and ultimately proved to be too much for the group. The group only authorized the purchase of 100 shares, with the restriction that one-third would be sold upon reaching a 30 percent gain, and an additional one-third being sold upon a 50 percent gain. The remainder would be held for an undetermined period of time.

Phillipe and I stayed home from school on the IPO day so we could track one of the largest purchases GRIG ever completed. I made the pancakes while Phillipe was online on my laptop, to make sure the trade went through. As 9:30 a. m. drew closer, the anticipation in our apartment began to grow.

Phillipe yelled to me, "The market's about to open! CNBC mentioned that our stock is one the market is looking out for!"

"That's great!" I said, sniffing the milk to make sure it was still good enough for consumption.

"Yeah! The market's open! Can you feel the excitement?" Phillipe quipped. Soon, though, our blood pressure would be sizzling, just like the pancake batter I was pouring on the griddle; Phillipe found out that we would be paying $40 per share instead of the expected $20!

That's right—the tech IPO curse hit us. Unprecedented demand for Earthweb forced the IPO price almost 100 percent higher than what had originally been expected. We salivated at the idea that such pent-up demand forced the price as high as it did. I immediately asked Phillipe if we should rethink the purchase. He said we'd be okay, as the group had voted for the purchase with the restriction of how many shares we bought, not the price at which it would IPO.

For both of our sakes, we hoped our analysis of the situation would lead to sure profits.

We tuned into CNBC until at least 2:00 p. m. that day, as Earthweb went on a roller coaster ride. It traded up and down all day while being featured by the news media's financial analysts. It eventually closed up a few points, but not high enough to trigger our automatic selling points. We weren't out of the woods with the first major test of our trading strategy. Just as easily as it closed up a few points, it could have closed down, well below what we paid for it. We would be on pins and needles until we hit our first selling point.

As it turned out, our fears were justified, but not before we took our money off the table. Five days later, we sold one-third of the stock at $52, an additional one-third for $76, and 33 shares at $79. Twenty four hours after our last sale, we only held one share valued at $46—yes, it fell almost 50% in value in one day. We experienced total gains, excluding the one share, of 71 percent in six days. If we didn't have our selling strategy in place, the opportunity would have been lost.

Phillipe and I dreamed about how much money we were making while having so much fun. Now that I had planted the seed, I started to see how money could grow on trees, if you knew where to go. By working together, we were able to quickly change our organization to take advantage of the stock market. We were investing hundreds of dollars and netting thousands in the market. I couldn't wait each day to do it all over again; it was a rush like no other.

To recap, our portfolio value was $14,000 in July 1998, $20,200 in September, and by the end of December 1998, more than $40,000. And over this period, our monthly dues averaged around $1,800. Without doubt, we were on our way to striking it rich in the stock market. Little did we know that this was only the tip of the iceberg, the beginning of big things to come.

What I Learned
• You better like the people whom your group members look to as their ideological leaders—especially if they're the founders. That's because once a culture is established, it's very hard to change.

• You better understand what you're doing. Any fool can make money in an up market, but only a smart person can make money in an indifferent or down market. To paraphrase Warren Buffett, America's greatest investor, the high tide raises everyone up, but it's when the tide goes out that you find out who's been swimming naked.

• Be willing to adapt to a changing environment. If the current way you're operating or communicating doesn't fit the situation, make the appropriate changes to keep the group moving forward.

• Taking accurate and detailed history of your group's actions is important. The notes should document both the good and bad actions of your organization, so the former can be repeated and the latter avoided and thoroughly learned from.

• Education is the best policy. The more you know about what you're doing and what you expect, the better decisions you can make and the faster you can grow. The faster you grow, the more involved your members are likely to be and, of course, you'll have more fun and make more money in the process!

Chapter 3
Weathering the Storm

Narrated by Ryan Williams

The ultimate measure of a man is not where he stands in moments of comfort, but where he stands at times of challenge and controversy.

—Dr. Martin Luther King, Jr.

Storms Ahead: The Tech Boom

Stormy seas—a fitting metaphor for any rough times in the business or investing world. Whether it's your own undoing and mismanagement, or simply a poor year for the markets, as we found out, you'd be wise to hunker down and have a strategy for weathering the storm until clear skies return.

Harvey yelled, "Vote passes, Ryan Williams is our new senior partner!" It had been only two short years since I joined

GRIG and I was already elected to the top position. Our operating agreement required that a new senior partner be elected
every two years. And although it hadn't been my original
intent, I found myself thrust into the spotlight with everyone
looking at me to keep the momentum—and of course, the
record profits of the group—going.

It just so happened to be a clear, sunny day in the summer
of 1999 when I was nominated to yet another leadership role:
senior partner of GRIG. Before joining the group, my full-
time responsibility was being a collegiate student-athlete with
little time for extracurricular activities. My everyday activities
seemed like a never-ending juggling act, consisting of eating,
going to class, attending tennis practice, attending group
meetings, studying and completing homework, only to wake
up the next day to do the same thing over again. But GRIG
changed everything.

It was amazing: our portfolio doubled in value and the
membership had an excitement that couldn't be hidden at
meetings. It was impossible to stop the craze of making even
more money and deep down, I even had moments where I
yelled, "Bet it all!"

It all seemed so strange. We started off with a diversified
portfolio that covered a variety of different stocks, from AOL
to P&G, Unilever, Bank of America, Iridium, Lucent, Agilent,
HP and so on. But I inherited the oncoming tech boom that
would eventually transform the investing world as we knew it.
Remember Tulip Mania? However, this time it was different.

Everyday, ordinary people became professional day traders
and boasted of their success based on hunches they had about

anticipating the next big dot-coms. The World Wide Web had caused worldwide hysteria and everyone—including young kids—was making money in the stock market. We had our own group of day traders who were ready to buy a stock and convince you that it was the best new Internet business, and it was going to revolutionize...*stamp collecting*?!

It was only a matter of time before GRIG's portfolio quickly transitioned to technology stocks. What had started out as a strategic, deliberate process of using models and analysis to select stocks turned into a flavor-of-the week decision-making process that loaded our portfolio with dot-com businesses. We were making so much money, we began to think that we were actually responsible for making it happen.

Monthly meetings consisted less of strategy and overall operations, and more of how much money we could make. Though busy in his day-to-day operations of managing his own business, Charles commented, "We need to be careful not to get caught up in the frenzy and think about an exit strategy that would allow us to realize gains, if necessary."

He also duly noted, "This trend can't continue forever." I vividly remember watching CNBC as he made these comments, and hearing famed investor Warren Buffett state that he was sitting on the sidelines during this time of unsustainable growth, and would not invest in anything that he didn't understand intimately, especially the non-proven business models of dot-coms. But, nevertheless, we continued to ride the wave and it was more fun than you can imagine.

By November of 1999, our portfolio had nearly doubled to $150,000 in just two months, and no one could tell us anything.

We had arrived and would be millionaires in a few years—or so I thought! Before we expanded our margin strategy, we decided that we first needed to determine what percentage of our capital structure, or portfolio value, we were willing to borrow against. Therefore, we all met, voted and decided that our capital structure was to consist of no more than 30 percent debt. This mechanism was put in place to ensure that we weren't overleveraged, and it ultimately controlled our thirst for buying more than we could afford.

However, this decision did not come without one of the many battles of GRIG versus Wendell. In round one, Wendell shouted abruptly, "I'm not comfortable with this idea and I don't think we should do it!"

Cooler heads prevailed, however. Harvey spoke out on behalf of the group: "Wendell, what is the problem?" As with most times when Wendell disagreed or held up the progress of group decisions, he didn't have a reason that he could communicate, or even a recommendation or alternative. However, his voice and uneasiness was to be heard, and he was willing to go to battle with the heavyweights of the group—and fight to the end if necessary.

I often asked myself, *Is he doing this because he wants to slow the progress of the group? Or does he just want his voice to be heard?* Finally, after minutes that seemed like hours of conversational bickering, quarreling, posturing and massaging, Wendell conceded that although he disagreed, 99. 9 percent of the rest of the group supported the idea. Democracy rules within a balanced and fair investment group. While one person may passionately disagree with certain decisions, a forum is provided for debate that shouldn't break out into fussing, arguing or fighting. Instead, it should lead to a decision that everyone can live with—one that maintains mutual respect for each other, hopefully!

Leading a Runaway Train

While not priding myself on being the most intelligent person in this group of young, motivated, brilliant individuals, they entrusted me with the opportunity to lead and leave my mark on GRIG.

Truthfully, I must admit, the decision to accept this role did not come without the influence of the founding father of the group, Phillipe. He did everything in his power to support my next steps and help relieve any uneasiness. I recall him telling me, "Ryan, it's not whether you're the smartest or are destined to be a leader. The personal growth you will get from taking on the responsibility of leading GRIG will be tremendous! Leaders are not necessarily born—they can be developed. We'll all be better for it! Your peers have selected you because they have faith in your abilities."

Enough, already! I stepped up to the plate. Phillipe had a way of influencing others that was unparalleled. I began to understand that the power was really with the group and not with one individual's skill set.

Nevertheless, I still questioned myself and my own leadership abilities. Was I really ready to take on such a great responsibility? Did I have the expertise? Did I have the time within my busy schedule?

When I was voted into the senior partner position, I sought support from two key positions: the junior partner, Charles, and the financial partner, Wendell. The junior partner would be needed for advice, guidance, direction and execution while the financial partner was key in managing and protecting our market-focused portfolio.

Charles was an individual who was highly respected in GRIG because of his advanced business acumen and experience as a real estate developer. During his term, he was managing his own company, which focused on building apartment complexes for universities.

As one of the youngest members, Wendell represented a challenge to authority and management—at least, until he was made to feel comfortable with whatever issues he may have had on that specific day. Certainly, he had less of a business background than most of us, but his tenacity and readiness to commit time, effort, energy and resources to the group earned him respect as a valued partner. It is the responsibility of all of us to speak truth to power and he was always willing to point out the cracks.

As I settled into my new leadership position, I really had no idea of what a roller coaster ride we would be in for. Stormy weather loomed on the horizon and looking back, I honestly wonder, was I ready for it?

A Family Affair

A family has disagreements, but at the end of the day, blood is thicker than water and they are able to still maintain love and respect for each other. GRIG operates similarly. While this may seem frustrating and unproductive to some, this is an important procedural process that groups will go through when making crucial decisions. It is best described as "a healthy dose of debate," which provides nourishment and growth to the group's collective soul.

Disagreements and differences can be interpreted as positive when they are intended to develop and move the group's aims forward. However, it is paramount that we remember—even in the heat of battle—that we are working together to accomplish the same goal. It should never become personal!

As each day and week presented huge gains accompanied by minor losses, Wendell who was the financial partner at the time, dutifully informed the group, "At our current rate of growth, GRIG's portfolio value will break the $200,000 mark within 30 days!" Naturally, we all rushed home from our day jobs and classes, and regularly checked our email in anticipation of reaching this momentous landmark.

Our portfolio was on a roller coaster ride, heading sky high, dominated by huge run-ups with minor dips. Every other day, we were breaking records in terms of one-day gains and, at the height; we saw a $15,000 increase in our portfolio in only 24 hours. We even received emails from members highlighting the latest breaking news on our portfolio.

Boom, Then Bust
As March of 2000 approached, GRIG was riding high along with every other speculator in the stock market. The NAS-DAQ—which was the exchange that included the majority of the technology-traded stocks—closed above 5,000 for the first time. While leading the group during this prosperous time, I began to think, *everything that goes up must come down.* How do we protect ourselves from getting caught in a bad position?

As anxiety started to keep me up at night, our market port-folio broke the $200,000 barrier as anticipated, and even shot up to over $220,000. Unknowingly, we had exceeded the 30 percent margin capacity that we had set for ourselves, and were currently at about 40 percent. This represented approximately $80,000 borrowed from our broker to fund our technology purchases. The wave, like a tsunami, was over our head.

Early April of 2000 marked the beginning of the end of the market's unchecked, unsustainable run-up. Within a two-week period, GRIG's portfolio lost over $30,000 in value. Just like deer caught in the headlights of a car, we all watched our portfolio of tech stocks plummet. What happened to our informal exit-and-sell strategy? Were we shell-shocked? Maybe, just maybe, this was a minor setback and the market would recover…or maybe not.

All good things come to an end, and on April 14, the mar-ket crashed, after a week of losses, with one of the largest one-time drops in history. The DOW fell 617. 79 (5. 6 per-cent) to 10,305. 77, the highest ever point total loss (the fifth biggest percent loss). The NASDAQ fell 355. 49 (10. 7 per-cent) to 3,321. 29, and the S&P fell 85. 78 (6 percent) to 1,354. 73. The tech bubble had officially burst.

Investor Lessons Learned
Investors in the stock market, along with the members of GRIG, watched in amazement as the storm continued to rage. We opted to maintain the wait-and-see approach to investing. This passive strategy proved unsuccessful and, to add insult to injury, GRIG started to regularly receive margin calls to cover the debt we borrowed from our broker. This meant that GRIG had to sell and liquidate stocks in huge amounts in order to maintain its portfolio.

Like a balloon losing air, the energy and morale of the group deflated. I wondered, *is there anyone to blame for this debacle?* As a leader, I took responsibility for not managing the situation appropriately, for not taking control and not making decisions to minimize the pain. Disregarding our original plan to buy and sell stocks wasn't worth crying over spilled milk or pointing fingers. Instead, we decided to focus on lessons learned:

1. Don't get caught up in the hype.
2. Diversification is important across asset classes.
3. Understand intimately what you're investing in and analyze it carefully.
4. Don't over leverage yourself.
5. When everyday, average individuals start entering into investments on a speculative level, with no specialized knowledge or advisement, BUYER BEWARE!

After the Storm
The group needed to ask itself, "Where do we go from here?" The partners had watched their capital accounts increase to unprecedented levels, and then sadly seen them destroyed.

Phillipe always talked about creating our own money tree and utilizing collective economics. He said that by working together we could leverage our skills and talents to create an organization that would produce wealth for all members. But, it looked like our tree was dying a short death, and was being replaced by blank stares and quiet meetings. This didn't seem like a story book scenario and I was getting concerned about the future of GRIG.

Everyday conversations with co-workers and friends turned into depressed accounts of how much money we'd lost during the tech bust. One co-worker, whom I considered a financial genius, expressed his utter disgust and mentioned how he had lost the shirt off his back and didn't know how his family would ever survive. I remember seeing him a year later, having lost most of his retirement savings and looking for new employment. I thought to myself, *what a disaster for him and his family*.

During this period, the average partner lost 50 percent of his capital account and, while despairing, a light bulb was also turned on. If we individually lost the amount of money GRIG lost in the stock market, we would each be financially set back for years. Just like my co-worker, we could have lost the shirts off our backs—not to mention kids' college tuitions, savings accounts, retirement funds and so on. Who honestly knows what other consequences would have come from losing this amount of money individually?

However, because we were investing as a group, the losses and risks were spread across it collectively, and the financial impact and burden were dramatically lessened. The collective strength, along with the will and perseverance of the group, would ultimately allow us to weather this devastating storm.

However, we didn't escape this experience totally intact. In addition to losing a significant portion of our portfolio, we lost a few members—including one of the founders. However, I began to truly understand the awesome power of collective economics and realized the potential of GRIG. If we were able to overcome this tough time in the group's history, this would bode well for a long and prosperous future together.

Annual Meeting After the Storm

The annual meeting was quickly approaching. It was scheduled to take place in August of 2000 in a rural, wooded location on the outskirts of Chicago, Illinois. Charles' family owned a vacation trailer there, and he graciously offered to host GRIG members for the meeting.

As I prepared to speak at the meeting, the pain of the past few months' events haunted me and I didn't know exactly how I would address the group. I realized that the storm wasn't quite over yet. We were just licking our wounds and beginning to look ahead.

Finally, the big day arrived, and we gave each other our traditional handshakes, hugs and kisses, as though we were at a family reunion. For the majority of us, this was the only time we got to see each other face-to-face, reaffirming the commitment and love we all had for GRIG; otherwise, we wouldn't have been in the middle of the woods talking and planning our future legacy.

As we began to review our past year's results, everyone listened intently. Instead of focusing on the doom and gloom, we talked about how we could ensure that we didn't repeat mistakes and what we could do to move the group forward. This positive and reassuring conversation let me know in an instant that the group had the character to overcome any challenge it might face! I recalled, Dr. Martin Luther King, Jr.'s famous quote: "The ultimate measure of a man is not where he stands in moments of comfort, but where he stands at times of challenge and controversy."

As nightfall set upon us, we all squeezed into Charles' trailer and concluded the first day's agenda. We began to relax and enjoy drinks, food and fellowship. Little did we know, we would have our first memorable annual meeting story for the year.

One of our most soft-spoken partners, who shall remain anonymous, after a few drinks, began a tirade: "[Expletive], I can't take it anymore! What is the matter with this investment group! I'm fed up that we move so slow and aren't making millions yet."

We all looked at each other, astounded, not sure if this was an Oscar-worthy performance or if it was real. This usually timid member continued with, "Am I the only one who is [expletive] upset with this loss?" He proceeded to lambaste the group, and then went outside to sulk further in his fit of anger.

The room was silent. While I must admit that this was one of the funniest impromptu outbursts I had ever seen, I was also concerned with what caused it, and how this person really felt. Once he calmed down, I went outside to listen to his concerns. He once again expressed his frustration with the group and apologized for the outburst. I tried to console him by preaching lessons of patience, and of the trials and tribulations necessary for success of the group, but my words were rendered inconsequential.

Unfortunately, this partner would eventually leave GRIG. I later found out that he was under a lot of stress and felt pressured to leave the investment group for financial reasons. I'll always remember a poignant thought that entered my head:

He'll one day regret the decision to leave this group. If he only had the vision to see our power and potential, he would persist and stay the course.

As we all know, life is about making decisions and I ultimately had to respect the decision this individual made. Many investment groups will encounter similar situations with partners who, for whatever reasons, may part from the group or may become inactive. But, the success and resilience of the group will ultimately depend on core members who have internalized, and are committed to, the vision and mission of the group. These members will step up during trying times and lead the group to the next mountain top.

At the conclusion of the annual meeting, we all said our goodbyes and departed, ready to write the next chapter in the history of GRIG. After this, the group experienced its longest period of inactivity as it regrouped, healed and planned for the future. My thought process as the leader during this time of inactivity was to perform a SWOT (strengths, weaknesses, opportunities, threats) analysis on the group and come up with a plan to optimize our strengths and opportunities, while minimizing our weaknesses and threats. During this time, I told Phillipe that the group needed to be stabilized. He agreed, and began to gear up to reassume a leadership role.

Leadership and Teamwork
It was also during this time that I reflected on previous leadership experiences and lessons learned. As a freshman entering FAMU in 1994, it had become abundantly clear that teamwork was part of life. While not one of my favorite things, it was a necessity in order to get tasks accomplished academically and athletically.

As a freshman, my tennis team had lost one of our most valuable leaders and players to poor grades, and I found myself thrust into a co-captain's role. I was unanimously voted in due to the respect I earned from my teammates, even though I was young and inexperienced. As a result, our team excelled, and we won the conference championship that year. Then, a few years later, I became the captain of the tennis team.

The lesson learned through this experience had not been about individual accomplishment. Collegiate tennis is based on a team concept, and a team was only as strong as its weakest member. Therefore, it was in your best interests to be your brother's keeper. My experiences in GRIG mirrored this concept.

I can't say I was a natural born leader or that I intentionally set out to lead others, but my peers and life experiences continually presented me with these opportunities, just as GRIG did. I was not always satisfied with the outcomes of situations while in leadership roles; however, each one was a valuable learning experience. I have since learned that excellence in leadership is a journey, not a destination.

I never yearned for the spotlight or needed attention, but I prided myself on being one of the hardest workers, leading by example, representing undeniable passion and willingness to play whatever role was necessary for the good and success of the team. It's important to have individuals with these traits when trying to build successful teams.

Moreover, I always self-analyzed the team and asked these questions: does the team need a role player? A motivator? A leader? What role can I play? This analysis was ingrained early on in my childhood and would be influential in my decision to take a leadership role within GRIG.

Teams exist to accomplish goals and develop reputations as winners. Therefore, it is important to have individuals on your team who have winning attitudes. Winning isn't everything, but personally, I absolutely loathe losing. Only through life experiences and being on teams have I learned how to appreciate the gifts of lessons in failure and losing. Michael Jordan wrote in his book, "Through my failures, I succeed."

While the allure and excitement of team activities were undeniable, one major concern for me was how I could possibly get individuals to accept responsibility and accountability for mistakes, and not make excuses for their shortcomings or losses. Ultimately, anybody can make an excuse and deny personal responsibility, and that's exactly what happened on numerous occasions during my tenure on teams. It frustrated me to rely on people who did not have the character to accept responsibility when they made mistakes or fell short of fulfilling their roles.

It is with this background and insight that I was introduced to GRIG in the fall of 1997, as a wet-behind-the-ears partner and investor, having no idea that I would be called on to eventually lead and continue to learn valuable lessons about leadership and teamwork.

My lasting legacy as the senior partner of GRIG was to recruit value-added members who would play an active role and allow GRIG to reach its potential. I've always had the ability to identify talent; I unofficially assumed the role of GRIG's number one recruiter, seeking out individuals within my network who I thought would buy into our vision of the group.

Ironically, as I began to share the group's goals with potential members, very seldom did I have to use pressure or sell the group to them. GRIG literally sold itself to these individuals, and I'm very proud to say that most of those who I referred to GRIG are intricately involved in leadership roles to this day. Little did I know that one of the individuals I would recruit into GRIG would change GRIG forever!

What I Learned

- Constructive debate is positive and necessary.

- Democracy rules within a balanced and fair investment group.

- The power of collective economics allows you to minimize (spread) the risk of loss while compounding the benefits of gains.

- Life is about making decisions, and the decisions you make will shape your life.

- Investment group members may come and go, but the success of the group will depend on a sound nucleus of members who have internalized and are committed to the mission of the group.

- Leaders aren't necessarily born, but they can be developed

- Leadership is a journey, not a destination.

- Your team or group is only as strong as your weakest member.

- Through failure, you can succeed.

- A good investment group will sell itself to potential members. Everybody wants to be a part of something great!

Chapter 4
Life After Death

Narrated by Marck Dorvil

"GRIG will be never be the same."

Rebirth

Phillipe's introduction:

I couldn't believe it. The group survived a very harsh time and—for a few minutes during the previous year—I knew we were in serious danger of coming apart at the seams. Certainly, it was going to take effort and some smart maneuvering to keep the wheels from falling off the whole operation. Losing 50% of our market value and getting a final report of the damage to our individual capital accounts for the year was hard to stomach.

Where did we go wrong? We had some of the brightest people in the group, yet we allowed ourselves to succumb to fast money and greed. My time as a general partner would soon be over and, as a founder of the group, I knew I needed to step up and help provide leadership to re-establish our direction. I talked with several members in the group to get support for a new team, and ran unopposed for senior partner at the next annual meeting.

I personally hand picked a team of individuals who were very loyal to my leadership style and devoted to the sustainability of GRIG. We ran on a platform of new direction and focus. This was the perfect catalyst for the rebirth of the group—a life after our virtual death. The group seemed ready for anything that would reinforce the principles and purpose from the first few years of our existence. We all somehow knew that it would work out, and that we would bounce back stronger than ever before.

Growth again emerged at the forefront of our unified determination as, even in a year of transition, new members became part of our vision. In fact, there was a new guy named Marck Dorvil and at the time, I didn't know the impact he would have.

I knew Marck from college, but only in passing. He was considered a strong and motivated worker, but I was skeptical. As a potential member going through the interview process, he asked more questions than others and seemed to challenge how things were done. Yet, he seemed well respected by most people in the group and couldn't wait to learn all the details of the ins and outs of GRIG. He also made it very clear that he wanted to be an active member and eventually become a leader.

I had to make a decision to either embrace this new guy or identify him as a threat to the organization. Some individuals are very strong-willed and can take focus and energy away from group objectives. It's important to understand the motives of people before

*you begin to embrace their ideas and give them access to the inner
workings of your organization.*

*The question of ethics and trust is also of the utmost impor-
tance, and making the call on any individual, especially someone
who will lead, can be the difference between survival and death.
So, I took it upon myself to call several people I knew who inter-
acted with Marck on a regular basis. After spending a few days
talking with them about his ethics, views and passions, I knew
that he was not only the right candidate for membership, but a
genuine leader. From what I heard, he had the tact and know-how
to get things done. One thing I knew for sure: if we brought Marck
Dorvil into the group, GRIG would never be the same.*

GRIG Would Never Be the Same, Huh?
How about I would never be the same. Phillipe had a way of
making general statements, but if you really paid attention to
them, you would realize that they really had a great deal to do
with you personally. And when I take you through my story,
you'll see why the transformation that was coming had as
much to do with the changes that occurred within me as it did
with GRIG.

It was the spring of 2001. I had recently graduated from
grad school and moved to Atlanta. I was a well-paid management consultant at a fast-paced boutique firm and was
engaged to my beautiful college sweetheart. By many accounts,
I guess you could say life was good. But, I was missing something I couldn't put my finger on.

All my life, I was always involved in some sort of entrepreneurial activity. I was always looking for some good idea I
could improve, develop or strengthen. As a child, I sold many

products door to door, and I did quite well because I learned how to take the sales presentations I was given and tailor them to the situation. For instance, if I was in an affluent neighborhood, my pitch focused primarily on helping keep a young kid like me off the streets and out of trouble. Meanwhile, if I was in an economically disadvantaged neighborhood, my pitch was more attuned to helping one of us get into college. I also figured out methods to better track and manage my revenues, expenses and inventory. That kind of creative thinking and process improvement mentality has stayed with me throughout my life.

I continued to sharpen my skills every year. In fact, I remember my first year in college, when I set up a very successful haircutting business in my dorm room. I noticed there were several students, including myself, cutting hair throughout the dorm. But everyone was doing their own thing. Everyone was competing against each other, and doing it very ineffectively.

It struck me that we could make more money working together than individually. I came up with an idea to bring several barbers together in one room, set standard hours, and leverage our collective equipment as well as expertise in different styles of cutting hair. I created a name, developed business cards and marketed the business through several creative outlets, including placing business cards in bathrooms. I figured, when you're doing your thing, you have no choice but to look straight ahead—and that's where you would see our card.

The marketing plans worked like magic, and the customers came in droves. I also made sure that we were always well groomed. I'm not only the president, I'm also…you get the picture. What better example to demonstrate our skills? I even found a way to keep the dorm personnel at bay by giving them free haircuts. Needless to say, the business was very successful and paid for many items that made my college life very pleasant.

I realized that I was pretty good at structure and organization. I also realized that I enjoyed it immensely. Later on in college, I took a fledgling mentoring program and brought it back to life by developing new and innovative outreach programs. I really enjoyed this project because of the connection I made with the community and the satisfaction I got from giving back to it. *Always remember your roots!*

After I passed the torch over to new leadership, I grew the mentoring program from less than 10 students to over 50, mentoring at not one but three different high schools. You may ask what does all this have to do with GRIG? Quite a bit, actually. These projects, among many others, helped set the stage for me to bring about change in a group that had not yet tapped into its true potential.

The Meet and Greet
Now that I've given you a little insight into my life prior to GRIG, let's go back to the spring of 2001—the year I joined the group. During that time, Phillipe didn't hold a leadership role. Instead, the person who ran the group was also the person who approached me to join it: Ryan.

By anyone's standards, Ryan is one of the most passionate and dedicated people you'll ever have the pleasure to meet. Ryan and I knew each other from our study session days back in business school. I always considered him to be a cool, calm and methodical person. I had a great deal of respect for him.

So when he mentioned he was running an investment group and asked if I was interested in learning more, I took it seriously. He mentioned GRIG's annual meeting in Atlanta and that it would be a perfect time for me to meet the group. We talked about GRIG and some of the good things—and not so good things—that were going on. As he talked, I listened. Then, it struck me like lightning—this was it! This was what I was missing in my life.

"So, are you down to come to the meeting?" Ryan asked me.

"Yeah, I'm down. Just tell me exactly when and where, and I'll be there."

I remember that meeting like it was yesterday. Back then, GRIG was an aggressive, small investment group trying to make its mark. The group didn't meet at any fancy hotels like we do today. No, back then, GRIG's annual meetings were held at any partner's house that was willing and able to host the event.

That first time I went, one of the group's members graciously hosted the annual meeting at her house in Atlanta, Georgia. I went with my wife, Janelle, who was my fiancée back then. I wanted to make sure she was involved in any decisions I made concerning our financial future.

We walked into the house and everyone was laid back, relaxing and eating barbecue. I immediately recognized a few folks I went to school with. I remember thinking; *This is my kind of crowd!* It was a bunch of young professionals in casual clothes, eating, talking about investments and just having a good time. I saw Ryan and walked up to him.

"What's up, Marck and Nelly?" Ryan said. "Glad you could make it. I told everyone you were coming, so I'm glad you're here."

"Not a problem, Ryan," I said. "I'm glad you invited me."

We gave each other assertive handshakes, and he hugged Janelle.

"We have a lot of food, so don't be shy," Ryan said with a big smile on his face.

"Don't worry. I won't." Of the many traits I've been told I possess, being shy is not one of them.

I remember thinking that the formalities of the annual meeting must have already taken place by the time Janelle and I got there. A few people were scattered inside, and several were outside by the barbecue pit. After mingling for a while, Janelle and I retreated to a couch and went to work on our plates of food. A few minutes later, I saw Phillipe. He must have been in another section of the house. We made eye contact and he approached me. "How's it going, Mr. Dorvil?" He had a hint of sarcasm in his voice, accompanied by a bright smile.

"If you want to be formal, I prefer sir or your excellence," I said jokingly.

I stood up and gave Phillipe a big hug, which was fitting since I hadn't seen him in years. Back in school, he and I never really ran in the same circles. We just knew of each other. I had a distant respect for Phillipe and all he was able to accomplish while still in school. I always thought he would be a cool person to work with. So to see him again, and to have an opportunity to be a part of what he put together, was great.

Like I mentioned before, Phillipe didn't hold any positions of power in GRIG at this time, which I found interesting. Although he was the founder, he managed to remove himself from a position of power and allow others to grow and build the group. You have to respect that in a man. That's the type of guy he was. I knew partnering with him would help me grow in many ways.

"So I hear you're interested in joining our group," Phillipe said, continuing with his slightly sarcastic tone. Phillipe was always jolly and this time was no different. I'm not sure if that was the way he had always been, or if he'd developed that as a way of making people relax and feel comfortable around him. Whichever it was, it seemed to work.

"Not sure, P. T. I have a few questions I need answered before I can respond truthfully. I'm sure you guys have a few questions to ask of me as well."

"But of course. As a matter of fact, we're going to get together in a little while to entertain new member applications. So, go ahead and finish eating, and meet us in the dining room in 10 minutes," Phillipe said as he patted me on the shoulder.

"No problemo."

"And who is this lovely person?" Phillipe asked as he shook Janelle's hand.

"This is my fiancée, Janelle."

"Hi, Phillipe, nice to meet you," Janelle said as she put her plate down and stood up to shake Phillipe's hand. Right then, Phillipe gave me one of those *You did good* looks and smiled back at Janelle. "Well, enjoy your food. When you're finished, make sure to mingle and meet all of the partners." He pointed to a group of people—Nkenge, Harvey and Wendell, who were debating the next big investment. He then left and returned to the crowd.

About 10 to 15 minutes later, we all gathered in the dining room. Several of the partners were seated near me, as well as Janelle and another potential member named Hendersohn Sudler. He later ended up joining too, and led the group's market investments team to double-digit results.

"I would like to call this meeting to order," Ryan said in a very authoritative voice. "We have the distinct pleasure of interviewing two potential members today, Hendersohn Sudler and Marck Dorvil. Many of us know these candidates and the value that they can bring to our group. Let's start by having introductions." The partners went first, and then Hendersohn and I introduced ourselves. Following the intros, the partners proceeded with questions such as, "Why do you want to join GRIG?" and "What value can you bring to the group?" Hendersohn answered first, and I answered next.

The next questions seemed somewhat strange. First, there was, "Are you ready to forget most of what your parents taught you about investing?" I also recall one question from a member named Wendell: "Do you believe that money grows on trees?" I was thinking, in the back of my mind, *What am I getting myself into?*

In time, I would realize the importance of all the questions they asked me. I never realized that an investment group would not only make money, but prove that working and investing together would get us further and faster than by ourselves. The money tree symbolized us getting away from the thought of things being out of our reach.

After the members asked their questions, Ryan allowed *us* to ask questions. Remember when I said I wasn't shy? Well, I didn't hold back with my questions. I asked about the current issues and concerns with the direction of the group, organizational structure, processes and procedures.

At the time, the group was going through a transition, having suffered a significant loss in the market. So, I also asked questions regarding its diversification strategy to help mitigate any future market fluctuations. In all, I probably asked a dozen questions, all of which the group did a decent job of answering. I knew there was a lot of work to be done, but I was up to the challenge. In my mind, I was hoping that the group was open to having me help shape its destiny.

Unbeknownst to me, elections were taking place during this annual meeting and Phillipe would soon be elected to the role of senior partner. Charles, a flamboyant and highly educated real estate developer, was chosen to be the junior partner.

I'm In
Soon after the annual meeting, I got a call from Phillipe. "Congratulations! You've been officially accepted as a full-fledged partner in GRIG." It was great news. He let me know that he was the new senior partner and talked to me about being a change agent. He asked for my assistance; I gladly accepted.

Only one month later, I got another call from Phillipe. This time, he was making a formal request for me to join the management team as the number two guy. Apparently, Charles needed to focus more on his own real estate development company and GRIG needed a competent replacement. I accepted the position, and the challenges ahead. I knew I was in good company and was energized to help move the group forward. I remember thinking that Phillipe had some grand ideas for the group, and now he had someone who could execute them. From that point onward, GRIG and my life became inseparably intertwined.

Change Is Coming

For the next two years, Phillipe and I worked in tandem as we reorganized and executed a host of strategic and process improvement initiatives. One of the first initiatives we implemented actually happened through casual conversation. I would like to say that it came about through long-range strategic thinking, but it didn't. The impact, however, was undeniable.

"Marck, you know we really have to get our hands on our accounts receivables," Phillipe mentioned to me one day as we discussed a myriad of GRIG-related topics.

"I agree. Do we have a target receivables range?"

"Not really. It would be great if we could get 100 percent of the partners to contribute their monthly dues on time."

I laughed, and put on my thinking cap. "Well, let's take a look at where we stand. Who's giving us the most problems and who are the folks who are always on time?"

Phillipe pulled up his spreadsheet and quickly shot out a few names. Immediately, I noticed a distinct pattern. The people who always paid their dues on time were on auto- debit. The ones who did not pay on time were not. There were a few who sent in checks on time, but they were not as consistent as the people on auto-debit.

The process of writing a check and mailing it in, and then having GRIG deposit it, could be very tedious, especially in today's hectic world. "That's it!" I said. "Let's require everyone to be on auto-debit. That way, it will make it easier for them to make payments and easier for us to collect them."

"I think that may be tough, but it might work," said Phillipe.

"Even if we convert just half, it will probably show a significant increase in on-time collections," I replied.

"Good point. I'll draft an email and send it out."

We noticed results immediately, and our large receivables account dwindled down to a very respectable level, allowing us to do more deals because we had more access to cash. In all, it was a quick improvement that yielded significant results.

However, not everything we did was as quick and easy to implement. We had a big issue surrounding the diversification of our portfolio. Because we had suffered a significant loss in the market before I joined the group, we were now in recovery mode.

One of the first areas I wanted to improve was our diversification strategy. I noticed that GRIG dabbled in a few areas other than the stock market. The group also speculated in real estate and small business opportunities, but we lacked focus. We needed to create a better system of working in these distinct areas. I suggested we create teams focused specifically on certain areas. This was the beginning of the next stage in GRIG's development—GRIG's new life.

I bounced the idea first off of Ryan. He was a structured and methodical guy, and I thought he might offer some tips on improving my idea. My motive was also a little selfish, as I wanted him to run one of the teams.

"Ryan, I came up with an idea," I told him. "We've been involved in several different areas other than stocks, and I was thinking that we should formalize it within a team structure. The teams I'm thinking of are ventures, real estate and market investments. Each team would have its own people, processes and budget to meet its objectives. What do you think?"

"Hmm, sounds like a good idea. It would give us a little more focus," Ryan said.

We talked at length, bouncing around several ideas. He made many good suggestions including having co-leads for each team, so the team leads could share responsibilities. It was a brilliant idea that would allow the teams to maximize their potential. This also created a succession path for the team lead. Later, we would formalize this into a full-blown succession plan for all GRIG leaders, to ensure the continued success of the organization.

As a quick note, the basic parts of the succession plan included:

- Identifying future leaders early.
- Clearly communicating requirements of the position.
- Providing the candidate opportunities to experience the role.
- Mentoring the candidate.

We also concluded that we needed to establish a support team for GRIG—one that was not focused on profits but more on our internal communication structure. We called this team "communications." The communications team would become one of the most vital parts of our success and eventually serve as the platform for one of our brightest partners yet—Vianka Perez Belyea.

Ryan and I presented this idea to Phillipe and the management team and quickly gained approval. Then came the hard part: execution. Ryan and I had a lot of work to do. I didn't know this at the time, but ours would eventually grow into a very tight and effective relationship, proving to be beneficial for both ourselves and GRIG.

It became clear early on that the first set of team leads, as they were officially known, had to be strong and well respected in GRIG. I proposed that Ryan take the real estate team and he agreed. We then discussed names and came up with a short list for the other team leads. At the top of our list for the market investments team was Hendersohn Sudler, who joined when I did. He had an incredible amount of knowledge about the stock market. We eagerly anticipated seeing what he could do with his own team.

The next team leads were Malcolm Jackson for ventures and Darien Swinton for communications. Both were intelligent and well respected in the group. We let the team leads select their co-leads as well as recruit their team members. Things were on a roll.

"I think this is a good list, Marck. I can't wait to see what the teams can do," Ryan said with a note of confidence in his voice. And just like that, we went on to create the team-based structure in GRIG.

But we weren't done yet. We actually had a lot of work to do. We had to help each team define its processes, from how it evaluated deals to how it made decisions on behalf of the group. To say that the team structure has been fundamental to GRIG's ongoing success is somewhat of an understatement. However, a team that isn't connected isn't really a team at all.

Therefore, to help facilitate the ongoing meetings of the teams and the general group, I found a Web-based conferencing service that enabled us to meet regularly at no cost. Since we were geographically dispersed throughout the US and abroad—a unique characteristic of our investment group—it proved to be an excellent tool for organizing and conducting meetings.

Another great resource was our revamped Website: www. grig. com. We recognized the need to improve our communication within the new teams, the partners in general and externally. To accomplish this, we hired a company to redesign our Website with a more professional and usable interface, to use as a promotional tool.

For internal partners, the new Website allowed storage and retrieval of documents, and the ability to post news and updates. It allowed visitors to learn about GRIG, submit online applications to join our group and post deals for our review. As spread out as we were, we needed to ensure that the right technologies were in place to give us maximum efficiency.

In addition, because of my background as a consultant, I was very familiar with process maps and flow charts. I recognized the benefit of graphically mapping out a process to represent visually what we wanted to happen when setting up systems, guidelines or procedures.

Visio was a favored tool of mine, though we could have also used PowerPoint or some other pictorial program. Ryan and I started on the real estate team first. We identified our process for investing in real estate deals in GRIG, summarized in the table below:

Step	Definition	Owner
Identify	Where to source deals	Sponsor of deal
Analyze	How to evaluate the deals	Team members
Decide	Yes/no or go/no-go decision	Team or entire group, depending on amount
Follow through	Communicate decision and if approved, ensure proper execution	Team lead, sponsor, financial partner

From that point, I worked with Ryan to map out a process of how deals came into and exited the group. We even developed supporting documents for roles and responsibilities, which clearly identified who was responsible at each phase of the process. Several other tools came about as a result of hashing through additional details. For example, we came up with a request for information (RFI) form to quickly and consistently gather information about a deal. The RFI asked several basic questions to help size up an opportunity. Basic components of the RFI included:

1. Brief description of the deal, including amount and timing for the funds.
2. Management experience.
3. Financing structure (percentage of personal investment versus debt versus outside equity).
4. Collateral being offered.
5. Projected return on investment and payback period.

We also came up with a scoring model to help balance the decision-making process. If the deal fell within a certain score, then it was a go. There were actually two models developed. One focused on short-term, quick-flip deals and the other on longer-term, cash-generating opportunities.

In addition to the above-mentioned documents, we developed a multi-part loan document to facilitate any loans we provided to potential investors. The loan document served the following purposes:

1. Gathered key information from the potential investor, so we could perform credit and reference checks.
2. Provided specific requirements for the loan, so the borrower was clear on our terms.
3. Outlined the collection policy, so the borrower was aware of payment procedures.

This tool also proved to be invaluable when streamlining our loan approval process.

I can't emphasize enough the importance of good organizational skills and a solid structure. These are instrumental in ensuring the achievement of an organization's goals. These documents, models and plans were integral and are highly recommended.

Yearly Review

Once we finalized the real estate team's process flows, we replicated the approach among the other team leads with variations, based on their specific needs. This resulted in a fully formed set of teams, overseen by team leads with support from co-leads.

The team concept was very successful. I couldn't have done it without Ryan's help. As the new team lead for real estate, Ryan went on to help make his team one of the most successful in GRIG's history, with record profits. That year, we invested in more than 10 real estate deals with annualized returns in excess of 120 percent. These deals were essentially investments in foreclosed properties that were bought with cash and sold for profit.

Years later, our focused team concept would allow us to invest in large multimillion dollar apartment complexes, create our own actively managed funds, and take ownership in many small business ventures.

Now that the teams were up and running, we needed a way to track and measure their performances. So, I created a yearly objectives review process. Essentially, the team leads would develop and present their objectives for the year to the management team. This gave everyone insight into what to expect for the coming year from each team.

The major components were as follows:

1. Develop a set of S. M. A. R. T objectives:
   -Specific—it's clear and unambiguous
   -Measurable—it can be tracked
   -Actionable—steps can be taken to execute it
   -Realistic—it can be done with available resources
   -Timely—it has a defined timeframe
2. Identify the resources required to accomplish the objectives. In other words, recruit individuals you want on your team.
3. Review and refine the objectives with management.
4. Confirm which members will be assigned to each team. I made sure members were allocated to a maximum of two teams. I didn't want anyone being stretched and not doing anything at all as a result. If you were assigned to a team, the goal was for you to be involved.
5. Package the objectives and team member selections into a PowerPoint presentation and distribute it to the group.
6. Start executing and measuring performance.

Not a bad process, but there was still something missing. One of the main concerns I had when developing the team-based approach was how to allocate funds optimally between the various groups to maintain a diversified investment portfolio. That answer came from Hendersohn, who proposed what evolved into the asset allocation model. It helped us not only determine how to best allocate resources among the group, but time our investments, estimate returns and project our future growth as well.

This was a priceless tool that the group would use each year in its review process. Moreover, the basis of the asset allocation model was to diversify our portfolio strategically, so that we were not over-invested in one particular area.

Ultimately, our real estate team was allotted the most funds, followed by the ventures team and then the market investments team. These allocations were based on risk versus return, expected deal flow and percentage to overall portfolio. We also allocated funds to the communications team, which supported the entire group. This asset allocation approach was done on a yearly basis and reviewed periodically throughout the year to ensure alignment in our investments.

Once we incorporated this new tool into our review, we shifted our focus to executing and measuring our performance.

During this "rebirth" and my tenure as junior partner, Phillipe constantly focused his attention on grooming me to be the next senior partner. He made it very clear that he would like to see me take the helm. He genuinely cared about the future of the group, and thus wanted to ensure its sustainability.

I knew that being senior partner was tough and demanding, and I had a great deal of respect for anyone who held that position. I also knew that I wouldn't be ready to it take over until I realized my process-improvement initiatives.

In my first two years as junior partner, I worked very closely with both Phillipe and Ryan to hammer out the critical issues in the group and bring about true change. When it came time for Phillipe to step down, I felt I was more than ready. And when I sat down to pick my new management team, I knew Ryan and Phillipe would be by my side every step of the way.

What I Learned
• Significantly improve your membership receivables by setting up an auto-debit process.

• Separate into teams based on investment objectives to help streamline activities and decision making.

• Have a succession plan in place to ensure your group continues to thrive.

• Employ technology, like a branded Website and free conferencing services, to improve your internal communication.

• Map out your processes and utilize tools like RFIs, scoring models and loan documents to ensure that you're working efficiently.

• Spend time planning your objectives and budget, and then track and measure performance.

• Utilize an asset allocation model to maintain a balanced portfolio

Chapter 5
Taking It to the Next Level
As Narrated by Phillipe Tatem

"I commit $10,000 over the next two years!"

I never understood what it meant to be committed to anything until I had to confront leaving the group I started. It was amazing that the organization continued to grow, adding more and more members each year, but there was something missing. It was the kind of hole that was too large to ignore, but hard to understand how to fix.

I was enjoying one Sunday morning with my wife and was discussing the family budget. She wanted to increase the distribution to my first son's college fund and employ a more aggressive strategy in paying off our school loans. We went over it line by line, and it was easy to see that one of the last things mentioned was our investment group, GRIG.

As the organization grew, I began to spend more time with it, taking away from quality time with my family and my nine-to-five job. How would this larger organization fit into my life? Were other members thinking the same?

I had a successful career as an executive at PepsiCo. My wife had her own career, and we had one beautiful child and were making plans for our next son. My family and job demanded time from me, and so did the organization. This is a question that faces most people in large organizations and in relationships throughout their lives. No man can do every-thing, and do only a few things really well.

I eventually made a decision that would once again refocus the organization and change what GRIG meant to everyone. You, too, will learn that small events have a tendency to make large waves. By the time the horizon is clear, it might be too late. Learn to read the small actions, to prepare your organiza-tion for the major shifts.

The biggest problem within the organization was keeping people engaged and active. As our members' lives became more complicated with demanding jobs, serious relationships and other challenges of adulthood, who had time for GRIG? We all believed in the mission of the group, but that wasn't enough to motivate members to spend the time needed to grow our organization.

As the founder, I was facing the same decision and knew the problem had to be resolved. GRIG was the last thing on our minds after work, childcare, high-priority family business and personal time. It was evident that the $125-a-month dues were not enough to get our attention. I was only paying $25 more a month than when the organization had been founded, back in college.

A look at some of Phillipe's household expenses:

Abridged Expenses

Cable	$98
Car	$293
Phone	$63
Utilities	$150
School Loans	$193
GRIG	$125

Our cable bill was almost as expensive as our monthly GRIG contribution. In our household, it was more of a distraction than a major investment. We were contributing ten times as much to our 401(k)s and other retirement plans, which required little work on our part and were producing average market returns.

The writing was on the wall: either get serious about GRIG or it would become less and less relevant in our lives. The long hours I had spent on the phone conducting GRIG business would eventually be wasted if we didn't do something. I put a strategy together that centered on making GRIG more relevant, and began to question other members: "Do you talk about GRIG at home?" My wife and I talked about the organization, but it was small in relation to everything else.

In the past, our group had attempted to classify members as either active or passive and had found a high correlation between the amount of money partners contributed to the group and the time they spent growing it. It was obvious that in order for GRIG to stay "center of the plate," we would need to increase monthly contributions aggressively, demanding more cash from partners.

I began polling members about their concerns and saw that I wasn't alone in this perspective, and that contributing more money and time was an issue many people struggled with. I soon realized that it wasn't just about cash, but about ensuring that we realized our potential and protected everything we spent time building.

Top four concerns of members:

1. Putting cash in and not getting it back out.
2. Clear strategy for success.
3. Reason to believe. Why now?
4. Improved financial reporting and transparency.

I called Marck, the senior partner that year, and expressed my concerns. He told me to put something together that could explain the situation. In his own way, he was confronting the same issue within his household.

"I was just talking to my wife about the same thing," he told me. "About how we can make GRIG bigger and make it have more impact than it has today. I love the organization, but we really need to take it to the next level. We need to consider doing bigger and smarter investments that produce cash flow. Corporate America can provide training and a steady paycheck, but true financial freedom lies in our hands."

It was indeed time for change. I told Marck, "I think we're fooling ourselves to think that this is sustainable, and that we can continue to attract the attention of our members with our investment strategy."

Marck and I spent hours, over several nights, talking about the future of the organization. Our wives joked that we spent more time with each other than with them. Those nights were very important in developing our change strategy and repositioning the group for continued growth.

The group's members would be presented with not only a strategy to commit more cash, but with a comprehensive plan to make GRIG a permanent part of their lives. It all made sense, when I allowed myself to think through the eyes of my childhood. We would seek investments that created cash flow and build wealth for our partners. Basically, we would internally grow our own money through investments that generated cash.

There was no reason to ask for more cash to invest in the stock market or a small business or two. But by altering our investment strategy to include equity ownership, we would change the group and double the cash we collected. We presented a plan to purchase and own businesses that would generate sustainable cash flow and provide profit distributions to members. That would be backed up by timely financial reports and a commitment by leaders to refocus with a renewed spirit. We identified several opportunities that we could invest in, including a bookstore, a veterinarian hospital and an upscale, full-service car wash and lube facility.

We decided to roll out this new strategy at the next meeting. The leaders were nervous about asking group members for larger cash contributions and laying out how the cash would be used.

We created a path for partners to make binding commitments to the group, with two years to honor those commitments.

Marck and I developed a calculator to help members decide how much to give based on the money they earned. We also had a form for members to sign, agreeing to our new strategy and their financial involvement. It was going to become a formal signing ceremony.

Commitment

Marck and I were second on the agenda to present our new strategy. The parliamentarian, Wendell, called the meeting to order. Then, it was our turn.

After our presentation, I asked, "Okay, members, now that you heard the plan and strategy, who is going to commit first?" Complete silence. I wondered if the whole plan had backfired, and if the idea was premature.

In the spirit of leading by example, I loudly declared, "I commit $10,000 over two years."I couldn't believe what had come out of my mouth. Was I losing my mind? I hadn't even asked my wife yet. On the other hand, it felt so good to say those numbers. The room became even more silent, if possible.

Before I resorted to pleading, Harvey stood up and said, "I will do $10,000!" And then Ryan said, "I will do $10,000!" Soon, the whole group was yelling out dollar amounts and we maxed out at over $90,000 in commitments from the 25 members in attendance.

The experience was surreal. It reminded me of a time when I was in church and the pastor asked the congregation for money to add to the building fund. He waved his hand in the air and said, "I pray that you have it in your hearts to contribute to the building fund, that you will allow God to work through your hands and that everyone who contributes would be blessed 1,000-fold." Although I'm not a preacher, I was thinking the same thing of my GRIG members. We were committing ourselves to breathing new life into a positive force that would benefit members and future generations.

As I recalled this event, Harvey reinforced the sentiment of all members: "Making GRIG relevant is more about ideas than about cash. It's obvious that the members' love and pride for the organization is real, but putting up money with no ideas would end up equally as devastating. Phillipe, Marck and our leaders have provided us with a new direction, and we all have accepted the challenge. Let us continue after this meeting by giving our time."

After the meeting, I talked to Craig Robinson—one of our members, who later became the largest financial contributor to the organization. Up to this point, he had contributed the minimum required, like most members, and enjoyed the social and educational aspects of GRIG.

However, Craig never really saw GRIG as being a serious piece of his retirement. He was moved by our vision for the future and made a $5,000 commitment during the pledge session. However, the events impacted him at a personal level and he would soon become another major influence in the group.

Measuring the impact of change is sometimes best told by those who are transformed.

Feedback from Craig:

> When Phillipe laid out the strategy, I was immediately sold. I was an outsider to most in the group and never went to a four-year college like most members. I was a proud product of Leo High School, an all-boys Catholic school in Chicago. I then obtained a technical degree because the price tag of a four-year college was beyond reach. I quickly became licensed as an operating stationary engineer and joined Local 399.

> I'm not that savvy in investments, but I learned so much from my experience with GRIG. I understood exactly where the organization was going and how that could fit into my overall retirement strategy. I joined the group like most of the original members, through a relationship with the founder. We played basketball and other games growing up on the south side of Chicago. I never knew the organization would last so long or that I would sponsor a $1.5 million real estate project on behalf of the group.

> But before I get too far ahead of myself, I would like to talk about the commitment meeting and how it changed me to become GRIG's number one equity owner.

> We all have to ask ourselves, *When do I plan on getting serious?* My government benefits were nice, but I

just knew that the talent that GRIG brought together and the spirit of commitment demanded that we make great things happen. I'm a saver by nature and decided to use GRIG as my second piggy bank.

The power of collective investment has never been more meaningful and yet so foreign to me. Most people in the group were okay seeing GRIG as another investment within their overall savings strategy. However, people don't realize that they have more control over what will happen to them in the next decade than they think. We sit around and get so comfortable in our environments, and we work hard to retire.

As a single man, my focus was on what I could do for myself. It was just plain unnatural for me to think that pooling cash with others could get me ahead. It is hard to put your retirement or your livelihood in the hands of other people, but we do it everyday—it just comes with a nice brochure and a song-and-dance commercial on television. We are fooled into thinking that we have a sense of security, but the reality is that Social Security, pension plans, 401(k)s, 403(b)s and big government might not help us.

I hear some of my union friends talk about jobs going overseas and corporate downsizing. You don't have to look far to see the cost of health insurance going up while the security of pensions is on the decline. It's a scary world out there, and among all that chaos, there are a few hundred people trying to sell you something.

It made total sense when GRIG put together a plan that would allow us to have more control over the outcomes of our investments. I'm not an investment banker or a big-time lawyer; I needed someone to help me figure this out without trying to sell me something. To support the purchases of businesses and other big bets, I put my money where my heart was: I tripled my monthly contributions to the group and put in more when I could.

This had an effect on me that I didn't know at the time. I began to participate in many group meetings and actually voiced my opinions. The leaders were right to say that money drives participation. I would suggest, though, that it is only part of the equation.

The vision of self-reliance and mutual benefit drove my decision and will continue to guide me and other members of the group. I think everyone out there needs to be involved in something like GRIG, so that they can make an impact beyond their perceived limited choices.

Craig's feelings are shared by many members. This power was unleashed shortly after our pledge to take it to next level. We had an opportunity to purchase a $1. 5 million multi-unit apartment building that, based on our internal analysis, would produce significant cash flow and profit for the group. We needed to raise approximately $250,000 in three weeks to seriously bid on the deal. We raised it in less than two by asking members for cash beyond their traditional capital contributions. The strategy allowed us to increase cash flow by $30,000 in the first year.

There were a few other notable changes to the organization to make accessing additional cash from members a reality:

1. Creation of co-investment agreements.
   - Allowed members to invest alongside the group, receiving full profits and principal back.
2. Incentives for partners who gave more cash.
   - Additional ownership shares for those who helped fund deals.
3. Incentives for members to source deals.
   - Shared profits and losses for deals brought to the organization.

The changes helped GRIG increase its cash position and changed the organization's approach to investing. We began to focus on larger investments that were well funded and had great chances of success. We went from investing $1,000 or $2,000 at a time in the stock market to investing $50,000 to $200,000 in many asset classes.

Preparing an organization for that type of change was no easy task, and ensuring that we had proper controls was even more important. It was understandable that when people began to give more dollars, transparency, controls and reporting had to improve. This was a critical success factor that made our organization great and increased members' trust in the operations.

A decision can't be made or funded without following proper procedures. There have been instances where we did NOT make lucrative investments in order to ensure that processes were maintained. Maintaining order helps create a secure investing environment within the organization, as this allows people who are not in charge still to feel comfortable with its operation.

During this time of transition in the group, I always remembered the early teachings that had inspired many members to join. Taking it to the next level became the theme of our annual meeting that year, and the dedication and sacrifice of members made it happen.

Early on, we had members who did without in order to support the organization's objectives; no great things can happen without sacrifice. Members would soon take risks and make decisions in their own lives as to how far they could go with collective economics. They took risks that could put their futures in jeopardy or cause temporary strain on their standards of living.

We lost some members that year as people decided that the sacrifice was too great for them. Imagination and dreaming is an American quality; hope is something that keeps many of us going. We placed hope in each other and imagined what was to be. Without any doubt, it was hard. It was a struggle to give up the pleasures of life in hopes of having a better tomorrow.

We were building a legacy that went beyond investing and profits. Don't get me wrong—those things are important. However, taking it to the next level is about "reaping what you sow." An organization is what you put into it…and it was time to turn that up a full notch.

Our records are an open book to all members and questions about credits and debits are quickly addressed. This is paramount to running a successful investment group. The perception of wrongdoing is equal to criminal activity when dealing with members' money. I would advise any investment group to establish ways to summarize the financial activities of the group and be prepared to explain all actions that the group takes.

The biggest asset an organization can have is the member who is willing to give more time. We benefited the most from Ryan. He dedicated so much time to the organization that people used to joke that he went to his corporate job to do work for the group. We even had his schedule mapped out: a 9:00 a. m. arrival with GRIG business starting at 9:30.

This wasn't really the case, but his dedication was so visible that people couldn't imagine him having the time for anything else. With focus and a drive for results, almost anything is possible. Taking it to the next level means giving time, not just cash. Ryan did both, and the organization benefited from his talents.

I always ask Ryan, "What motivates you?"

"Passion and love for the group motivates me," he answers "I have passion for not only what the group stands for, but for the people that are in it. I put in many hours to review business deals, help members with financial literacy and develop a platform for wealth building because I know it will pay dividends. I wasn't always a leader in the group, and I even thought about how serious GRIG was to me. I committed more cash to the organization, but without time, does it really matter? I view GRIG partners as an extended family. It has to be personal."

Managing time in an era where it is so difficult only comes from a drive to get it done. The biggest thing I hear from people is that they don't have the time to deal with a bunch of people interested in investing. This is not for the lighthearted. I value more highly the member who gives time than the one who shows up with a paycheck. It's amazing how much time opens up when you commit to something.

When I couldn't get a chore done, my mom used to say, "If you wanted to get it done, it would be finished by now." That is so true. More importantly, when you have love and passion for an activity, it's no longer work—it's fun! You do the things you want to do and delay those that are less interesting. People tend to be satisfied with living in a society where most things are at the end of a remote control or accessible via a drive-through window. Financial freedom is something that you have to demand for yourself and work for.

Ryan usually can move the casual listener with his passion. However, it is this willingness to give time that is so important for any organization to survive. The average member gives two hours of time to the group per month. When it comes to people in leadership positions, it can be as high as ten hours per week.

Based on our poll of other investment groups, time commitment from members can be less than an hour a month. All members aren't required to participate in all meetings, but we have the expectation that everyone will give when relevant. To quickly address issues, we have a policy stating that passive members who fail to show up for a vote are not included in the count. This gives extra encouragement to attend a minimum number of meetings to maintain active status. Additionally, it allows our organization to remain flexible and act on opportunities.

What I Learned

• Making sure the organization stays relevant for members is one of the biggest challenges for leaders.

• A clear strategy for success and knowing how much money it will take to get there will rally the troops.

• Ensure you have both short-term and long-term incentives for the membership, or those who can't wait will leave.

• Financial transparency drives increased contributions; make sure your books are easily understood and always open for review.

Chapter 6
Get Active, Stay Active
Narrated by Vianka Perez Belyea

"Members are an organization's strongest asset."

I remember it like it was yesterday: I picked up a 2003 issue of *Black Enterprise* with a lot of excitement. Many will not be able to relate to this experience, but it's one of the things I look forward to every month; there's something to be said for loving to learn. *Fast Company* and *Fortune Small Business* are two others; these publications really challenge how I think about being more effective and productive. I am always looking for a better way to get things done.

However, I wasn't always like this. Actually, it didn't start until my second professional job. After working there for almost two years, I was struggling with the feeling that I was not being challenged enough, and didn't have the power to change really basic things that impacted my department. Worst of all, I started to lose confidence in my abilities as an employee. I constantly questioned myself: *Am I smart enough? Would I be able to succeed in a corporate environment?*

Given my situation, and thinking about my career and next steps, I then asked myself: *Do I really want to have a job for the rest of my life? Do I want to depend on an employer to have financial stability?*

I wasn't raised by my parents to ask these types of questions, but given the corporate environment of today and how different it was 15 years ago, how could I not?

It wasn't until one night when I had dinner at a restaurant in Boston with Tavinder, a good friend and co-worker, that I experienced a shift in the way I perceived Corporate America. As an MBA candidate, Tavinder offered some insight on various business models, and I always had something to contribute from the many business books I read.

It was clear from the beginning that we were both very driven and entrepreneurial. Over antipasti and wine, we talked about our dreams and the importance of financial independence. At that time, I was considering starting a frozen dinner business and asked her if she was interested in being my partner. Although it didn't come to fruition, it opened the door to the possibility of other ideas and projects that we would entertain as business partners.

Cultural Transformation
During this personal growth process, I realized that it was important for me to focus on an area that I not only felt I was

good at but that would be beneficial to the organization. Levering the organization as a whole, and constantly thinking of ways to create an environment that was conducive to teamwork, professional development and education, were things that I was very passionate about. Of course, strategy and finance are as crucial to the success of every company, but, for me, I knew that any major efforts that I committed to would have to recognize people as a major asset.

So when I turned to the "investment club" page of the April 2003 issue of *Black Enterprise*, I didn't realize that GrassRoots would be the organization that I would soon join, or that I would become part of implementing a philosophy that I truly believed in. For me, the initial focus wasn't about wealth building; it was about regaining my confidence. GRIG came at a perfect time because I didn't have to leave my job to participate in projects that would challenge me. Within a month of joining, I was considered an active member.

Initially, I became involved as the co-lead for the real estate team, as a way to test the waters. I had thought about investing in real estate in the past, and this was a good opportunity to learn more about the business. Plus, I wanted to learn how members worked together and how management made decisions.

We entertained some great deals during this time, but there really was no process flow in how we evaluated upcoming deals. I worked with Ryan, who was the lead, and he was depending on me to put some structure into the real estate team. But it was really Marck, the junior partner at the time, who drove this initiative.

Although the process was tedious, involving mapping every step on Visio, it turned any complicated deal into very straightforward steps. Very few deals went belly-up as a result. And yes, we could not control the real estate environment, but the process did allow us to take calculated risks. Marck was able to execute process-flow initiatives successfully across all the teams with minimal pushback, and with significant support from management and team leads.

Communications

Overall, my beginning at GRIG was a rewarding experience, just as I hoped it would be. I spent about one year on the real estate team and then moved on to the communications team.

It was appealing for two reasons: the communications team lacked any tangible credibility within the organization, mainly because it didn't provide any revenue, and I wanted to see if I could change the role of the team within the organization, creating a culture that would impact the organization as a whole. It was a true test for me, and exactly what I was looking for.

Only the management positions were elected by the partnership; all others were appointed by the senior partner. I remember having a conversation with Marck, who was full of excitement. He had joined a year before I had. We really wanted to make a significant impact, and identified ways to accomplish that.

There was no doubt in my mind that Phillipe was grooming Marck to be the next senior partner. Marck definitely had the skills and gained alignment with key people in the organization. He knew not to take this for granted, because unlike his experience at Home Depot, where he worked during that time, a majority vote was necessary for all major decisions, including voting him in as the next senior partner. And when he became senior partner, I was one of the first people he asked to become a team lead.

I'm not in the minority when I say that Marck was difficult to tolerate initially. His thought processes were external and very detailed. A question was usually followed up by a comment and a question, and then another question. You could see the facial expressions of everyone around the table saying, "Here goes Marck again!"

Although many of us, including Marck, were not able to recognize this early on, he changed the thinking paradigm of how GRIG did business. Now, the "Marck questions" are asked and answered within the teams, and each lead is expected to come up with a thorough proposal for new initiatives.

In my first year as a communications lead, it was immediately obvious to me that the team lead had very little control and that management made the big decisions. I remember talking to Wendell about this. We had many conversations, but I remember one night when we talked for two hours about the history of the team and the fact that it didn't have a strong leader. He had been a member since the beginning, and his perspective and insights shaped the steps I took to change the team's image.

We all know people like Wendell. He is extremely committed to what he does; he's a strong voice for the minority; he goes by the book and can be a pain at times. Every company, department and team has someone like him. Yet, every person has strengths and weaknesses. The question is, who will best fill the role for what needs to be accomplished?

We all know how it feels when we're asked to work on a project that doesn't really match our strengths, but more important is the inability of our bosses to make this assessment properly. Ineffective people are often put in the wrong places.

There was one time when we proposed eliminating the member level, which contributed a lower capital contribution than partners. Wendell wasn't onboard, and we were all very frustrated with him. We had been on the phone for two hours already and were close to agreeing to only allowing partners to join, which would be financially beneficial to GRIG. But, every point Wendell raised made us think more carefully about the decision we were about to make.

Wendell tends to align himself with anyone who thinks of the organization as a whole, rather than the top ten GRIG stakeholders. As the former parliamentarian, he always goes back to our operating agreement to ensure that we make decisions in a fair and equitable way.

Direction of Communications

It was important for me to get Wendell's support in the development and advancement of the GRIG communications team. We both agreed early on that it was vital to identify the team's role within the group. We scheduled several brainstorming sessions and came up with the following:

1. Be the main vehicle for communication, internally and externally.
2. Provide marketing/PR support.

3. Engage and involve the membership.

4. Support other teams in creating policies and procedures.

All four tasks were major challenges, since they required changing how things were previously done. I had full support from management. Now, the senior partner, Marck and I were aligned on these objectives, and they became the pillars of the communications team in the following years.

Energizing and Engaging

I had some wider exposure to the team as part of the Annual Meeting Committee. I joined the committee for personal reasons—I love traveling and wanted to find locations that I would be interested in seeing. I knew my husband, Aaron, was initially excited as well, since I wouldn't have to drag him to all those places I wanted to visit!

Moreover, I saw the annual meeting as one of the ways to get the group motivated and energized. In the past, management did 65 percent of the work. I knew this model would eventually collapse if we continued to grow at the present rate. It would, without question, hinder our potential.

The group entertained many options for getting members engaged. However, our efforts were scattered. This is not to say that the approach needed to be the same across the teams, but that we needed to identify a process.

Before doing that, changing the culture of our organization was necessary. How could we do this? Could we accomplish it in a non-corporate setting? I didn't have anything to lose. It wasn't something I had the opportunity to do at any of the jobs I worked at before. So, why not?

A big step in the process would be recruiting some new blood. In fact, one of my greatest accomplishments as communications team lead was when GRIG was featured, for the second time, in the May 2006 issue of *Black Enterprise* as one of the "most successful investment clubs." It wasn't luck that we'd made the headlines again. We were very organized in our approach. As a result of the article, five new high-caliber members joined.

We expected the extra publicity to increase the number of hits from visitors to our website dramatically. In addition, the number of interested applicants would be more than usual; therefore, we planned accordingly. One of our members had a great idea to streamline and create consistency in the interview process due to expected increased demand from the article. I organized a core group to move this idea forward, including Marck, Ryan, Phillipe and Jennesia. The new interview tool became the instrument for evaluating potential members.

Questions included:

1. Skill compatibility: if you could join one of the teams (communications, market investments, ventures or real estate), which would it be?
2. Leadership and execution: name an initiative in which you have taken the lead, and walk us through the process of completing this initiative (resources, project plan, networking).
3. Time commitment and management: what other groups or activities are you involved in and how do you plan to balance your time with GRIG?
4. GRIG relevance: what are your short-term goals and how do you see GRIG assisting you in achieving them?

GRIG's recruiting process was revitalized by this new interview tool that we created. It allowed us to evaluate not just financial but also personal commitment. Half of the questions were aimed at the interviewee's interest in participating and contributing to the organization.

The goal was stated quite simply: to get the new members to realize that GRIG meant serious business when it came to giving time. More specifically, we didn't want new members to fall through the cracks. We wanted to connect them right away with the teams that most matched their experience and our needs. As a result of the interview tool, new members such as Cassandra Theramene and Michael Cox quickly found their niches at GRIG, becoming exceptional and invaluable members. They really hit the ground running.

As for engaging the larger group as a whole, that would take a little more work. Looking back, GRIG has been in existence for almost 10 years now. Although we've lost some good people, there is still a core contingent of original GRIG members. How would I get them to buy into the new GRIG?

As I mentioned earlier, our initial approach to increasing engagement was scattered. We developed a mentoring program that, to be honest, wasn't successful. Thus, at an annual meeting, Marck and I agreed that we would ask leaders to become more involved in reaching out to members on our inactive roster. The first step was to list all of the inactive members and go through each of them, one at a time. Through roundtable discussions, we put the inactive members into two groups: non-targeted and targeted.

The non-targeted inactive members simply did not want to be involved in any efforts of the group. They were comfortable paying their dues and letting others run the show. Students were also included in this category, as most of their time was dedicated to school. The targeted inactive members were those who wanted to be involved, but because of lack of communication and direction on our part, were disengaged.

Once this list was developed, we assigned the targeted inactive members to one of the existing teams. We then asked each of the team leads to identify a specific task that this person could be involved in, and to report to management quarterly on their progress. As a result, we have had the highest participation levels ever in the history of GRIG.

Meanwhile, we realized that there is nothing wrong with having inactive members who only contribute money. Without their funds, we would not be able to accomplish our goals at such a fast pace. But we all realized that not all inactive members wanted to remain in this category. Some just needed more guidance, a reason to become active. Another lesson we learned was that when you set expectations and measure progress, the outcome tends to be very positive.

Providing focus and rewarding performance were also key elements in getting members more actively engaged. It was clear that management wanted to move toward compensation based on achieving our objectives. In 2006, they committed to adopting a compensation model that would benefit the entire membership. This was no easy task, as there had to be some criteria to reward those who went above and beyond while not alienating members who were minimally engaged.

Members Come, Members Go

In preparation for the most recent annual meetings, Marck and I worked on finalizing the annual report, noting that we'd lost eight members in one year! We were excited about the five new recruits we'd gained, but we weren't positively sure of what had gone wrong with the eight who had left.

I asked Marck, "Do we know why they left?"

He responded, "I think Harvey told me that two were for financial reasons, and I believe one had to move out of New Orleans because of Hurricane Katrina."

Of course, people come and go; it's a fact of life and business. But it was clear that we had to get a better sense of why people were leaving. As a result, we started to work on a retention program, so that we would know why members left GRIG. It would also help us be more proactive in uncovering reasons why members might leave in the future. This gave us a head start on addressing the concerns and needs of our members.

We conducted a retention survey and asked questions such as:

1. What were the reasons why you joined GRIG?
2. What must GRIG accomplish in order for you to be satisfied?
3. What would cause you to withdraw your membership from the group?

The answers to these questions gave us insight into what steps we needed to take in order to retain valuable members.

Branding the Group

The great things about an investment club are that everyone has joint ownership, and mutual input is strongly encouraged and considered. Let's all think about our daily rat-race jobs and the idea that what our boss says goes. I have a full-time job where that's the case, and one boss is plenty, if you ask me.

GRIG management, dominated by three strong men— Phillipe, Marck and Ryan—was difficult to convince on some initiatives. Although they were supportive, we got into battles, some of which I strategically chose. Nevertheless, not all of the communication initiatives went smoothly.

For instance, one of the toughest battles, which I can gladly say I won a year later, was about branding the organization. I remember having a conversation with Marck, and recall that we were on the same page—until he talked to Ryan and Phillipe.

I received a frantic voicemail from Marck, who didn't sound too optimistic. I was at my friend Tavinder's house, going over our business plan, when I returned his call. I said to Tavinder, "This may take a while, and I need some privacy." I don't think she realized how business-minded we were until then.

I was quite upset when I got off the phone and the first thing she said to me was, "You have two full-time jobs, and you're the vice president at one of them." She was referring to GRIG.

The branding of GRIG was important in my eyes. I'm not the creative one, but thanks to my husband, Aaron, who is a graphic designer, I am now able to understand the power of marketing and advertising. He is brilliant at identifying what works and what doesn't. When I see billboards, it's no longer a picture of just a BMW—it's a thought-provoking tagline, a compelling use of color and, when implemented correctly, a clear overall message.

Sometimes I feel like I'm taking a test when I'm with Aaron. I would say that my GPA is a B+ in graphic design; I got extra points for remembering what he taught me about Pantone colors, but I needed to work on advertising subtleties. At his studio, Alphabet Arm Design, the designers worked on a wide range of projects, from marketing materials to creating an identity for a record label. Naturally, I asked him for his feedback on GRIG's branding.

He gave our overall branding a C+. I recall what he said verbatim: "Vianka, this logo is not built well. It doesn't feel distinct enough. Imagine sending this to *Money* magazine. It wouldn't print well. Also, it's not consistent with what you have on your website and business cards. Think about all the companies you admire, and what's the first thing you think about?" I went over the list in my head: Starbucks, Southwest Airlines, Benetton, eBay, Google. I wanted GRIG to have the same memorable and distinctive look and feel.

After the frantic voicemail, I spent a lot of time crafting the argument for Marck. The communications team had a very small budget, and although $1,000 was not a lot of money, I knew it wasn't going to be easy to obtain.

Marck was very strategic in his approach. He found a way to tell me that branding the organization, a new logo and marketing materials were not a priority, and that we couldn't justify spending $1,000 this year. I was pretty upset, because I had worked really hard to get to that point. I knew that he understood how I felt, or at least I thought he did. I came to the conclusion that Phillipe had played a role in the decision. He was an invisible CEO—he was there, but not really, and got his point across through other people.

I have a lot of respect for Phillipe, no question. He has been the driving force of the organization, and without him, I'm not sure where GRIG would be today. He has allowed all of us to be part of his vision. I can only imagine how rewarding it will be for him when members are reaping the financial benefits 15 to 20 years from now.

Certainly, Phillipe has a way of swaying people and one of his strengths is negotiating. You don't realize it's happening until the decision has been made. It's quite amazing to watch, and I had the luxury of being an observer for quite some time.

To his credit, GRIG had blossomed as a result of what Phillipe had done. I remember when he said at the 2004 annual meeting, "I want GRIG to be a discussion around the dinner table. I don't talk about it with my family because it's a small piece of my investment portfolio. We have to change that!"

One of his brightest ideas yet was creating a new category of members: principal investors, each responsible for committing an additional $5,000 a year. At every annual meeting, he goes around the room asking for people to commit additional money. No, it's not written on paper—members have to share their amounts out loud. So, are we talking with our loved ones about GRIG now? Absolutely!

My relationship with Phillipe has changed for the better. He comes directly to me when he disagrees with my decisions, and therefore no longer seems like an invisible hand, wielding power behind the scenes. I'll have to be honest and admit that at times, I do find myself relaying his message to others, too.

Eventually, I got my point across that branding would help us establish an identity permeating everything we did, and would be consistent in all our activities. It showed a level of professionalism that would appeal to firms and individuals who were interested in partnering with us on lucrative deals. The process wasn't easy, but by that point, I had gained enough credibility to call some of the shots.

The Power of Feedback

From my personal and professional experience, there is nothing that impacts a change in a person's behavior more than constructive feedback. I am a huge advocate of this; as my family and close friends know, I am constantly trying to improve and reinvent myself. I also expect this of others whom I care about.

For the eighth annual meeting, I proposed to Marck and Ryan a performance evaluation segment for the leadership group. It was clear what the rewards would be, but Marck and Ryan were a bit hesitant at first. Should we give feedback on what members could do better as GRIG leaders? Would they take it personally and not be as engaged? How would this be set up? I had to be creative...

Basically, I decided to split GRIG members into two teams: A and B. There were about seven people in each group. Both teams had to evaluate each member on two criteria:

strengths and areas of improvement. One spokesperson was selected to give the information on each member from the opposing team. It was initially stressful to facilitate these sessions, but to my surprise, each team was really into it. Ryan even asked that I stay away when I was being evaluated.

Harvey, who was the junior financial partner at the time, was on team A and the first one to receive constructive criticism from the group. Wendell, as the spokesperson for team B, spoke about Harvey's strengths, weaknesses and areas of improvement.

Of course, Harvey wasn't the only one who was tense when under the spotlight. You could read his mind, and the minds of others: *What are they going to say about me? How do I take this as constructive criticism?*

I don't think there were any surprises, although a few struggled with what was said about them. In a way, it seemed like some of the members were seeking constructive criticism to better themselves. Did I already mention that we contributed money and didn't get paid to be part of GRIG? It really hit home with this exercise how committed each of us was to the philosophy and spirit of GRIG's "together, we grow" approach.

This exercise was such a huge success that during the early stages of planning the following year's meeting, everyone asked if it could be added to the agenda! We were all excited to see if any personal progress had been made. I heard Marck saying, "I bet folks aren't going to say that I'm not as involved now." And Jennesia said, "I've definitely been more proactive this year."

For Marck, the feedback focused on his leadership skills; we all thought that over-delegation was an area he should work on. On the other hand, we felt that Jennesia should focus more on leadership efforts.

Since then, we have made feedback an integral part of our process, with modifications as needed. We've improved not just GRIG, but the individuals that comprise it as well, and as a result, members are the organization's strongest asset.

What I Learned

• An interview tool can be used to evaluate candidates in a consistent and equitable way.

• Member evaluation confirms what is being done right and focuses on areas that need improvement.

• Being proactive in retaining members is key to any organization.

• Engaging members is the responsibility of every person in a leadership position.

• Communication is one of the pillars to a solid organization.

Chapter 7
Realizing the Storehouse
Narrated by Phillipe Tatem

And God said, Let there be light: and there was light.
—Genesis 1:3

Not every organization is prepared for change, but change is a critical component of any successful and prosperous investment group. Being dynamic and always adjusting tactics to meet current demands separate the winners from the losers. GRIG has adopted a chameleon-like attitude and continually looks for ways to improve and drive results. Yet how does this have anything to do with the Lord?

Well, I was sitting quietly one Sunday morning, listening to my pastor preach, when something he said struck me. He quoted the following passage from the Bible:

"Bring the whole tithe into the storehouse, so that there may be food in My house, and test Me now in this," says the LORD of hosts, "if I will not open for you the windows of heaven and pour out for you a blessing until it overflows."

—Malachi 3:10

By our ninth year of existence, the organization had adopted a principle that was foreign to most people. This concept was the storehouse. As a group, we met most objectives we set out to achieve and had confidence in our future, but we were still very independent in how we approached our commitment to work together.

What I'm about to tell you is the biggest issue that faces people today, and if GRIG doesn't get it right, it will be our downfall as well. People talk about collective economics and working together, but the execution of this principle is usually far from perfect. It is a natural human instinct to look after yourself and your family at the expense of all else.

In America, where the unofficial motto is "look after number one," capitalism drives consumption and self-indulgence by reinforcing images of personal success and individual riches. There is nothing wrong with any of these ideals, but an organization built on true collective work and benefit cannot function without a divergence from these thoughts.

Thus, the storehouse came to be a rallying cry for our organization. The central idea was about bringing tithes into the storehouse, so that people wouldn't rob the teachings of Christ:

The members with money must bring it into the storehouse. The members with talent must bring it into the storehouse. The members with networks must bring them it into the storehouse.

And the list goes on...

However, like most passages in the Bible, Malachi 3:10 also had a hidden meaning for me. It was about being selfless and committing fully. When I heard this sermon, I immediately began to think about the organization I created, and its potential. One of the biggest challenges in any organization is keeping people engaged and focused. Well, we had the same problem, and hopefully, some of the tools in this book can help you manage those situations.

The one thing that will be beyond your control, but should be addressed, is the hearts of the members. Coming together was the easy part. Sustaining the organization and making it a legacy for future generations was much more difficult. It required the storehouse. Everyone on the team had to contribute what they could to achieve the group's objectives.

Another obstacle we faced was getting people to use these powerful individual resources for the benefit of the group, rather than themselves. This is the one thing that has stopped smaller organizations from being great. *Who would do it first?* one member wondered. *How do I personally gain from my contribution?* thought another.

All Created Equal: Building a Collective Mindset

When GRIG was founded it was based on all members being equal. This was a good start, but trying to keep everyone equal limited those who could do more, and put pressure on members who didn't have enough. It took some time for me to realize this, but the answer seemed so clear. The leadership restructured our organization, introducing new classes of membership to allow people to give significantly more cash and own more of the group.

We gave incremental ownership to those who contributed significantly to the group and allowed a level of membership that would be required to pay less than an average partner. Additionally, we had a heart-to-heart discussion within the organization that helped communicate GRIG's vision and attuned everyone to the fact that we needed each other. Literally, we were blessings for each other, and many of us didn't realize it.

The main question was, how could we be successful as a team if members were spending significant amounts of time collecting rent and handling issues related to real estate?

I remember a meeting called to review personal financial health. Each year, we conducted a survey that asked questions of our members about their personal financial health. In this survey, people disclosed some of the things they were personally investing in and how they used discretionary money.

The results showed something very strange: we all were individually investing in real estate and building personal real estate portfolios. This was completely counter to what the mission of the organization was about.

I remember calling partner Ryan Williams and asking him why he had four homes. His response would help set a new course: "I had a great opportunity to make some money and I picked up some undervalued homes to help build equity and create cash flow."

Most of you out there would say that there's nothing wrong with that! And yes, indeed, there are many books that tell you how to increase cash flow, purchase with no money down and make yourself rich. However, there are hardly any teachings that tell you the easiest path to increasing cash flow and riches is with your neighbor, and not by yourself. The saying "there is power in numbers" is particularly meaningful.

What we realized was that Ryan, Marck and eight other members were purchasing investment properties, and many of those members were experiencing headaches. They were spending time away from the organization to handle issues related to those investments, and we were quickly being de-leveraged.

The solution to this and many other investment opportunities in the group was to sell off individual real estate and build a portfolio together that would leverage the expertise of all members and allow us to collectively afford such an investment. Now, I won't say that everyone sold off everything, but I will say that people got the message. And as you read in previous chapters, we now jointly own large, million-dollar, multi-unit apartment buildings.

The biggest strength we have in GRIG is selling ideas and concepts, and understanding how to manage so many different personalities under one collective organizational umbrella. In my years in the group, I've observed three negative reactions to change:

1. "Blunt"

This is the easiest form of negative reaction to handle because a member or partner just tells you, "I don't like it and here is why." In the case of realizing the store-house, one of our leaders was spending significant amounts of time handling one full-time job and two investment opportunities. He said that having an individual portfolio was important and that GRIG was just a part of his strategy. Knowing where he stood, it became easy to address his concerns and explain how we could maximize his investments by working together.

2. "Great Idea, But…"

This is one of the worst reactions, because these people will agree while quietly undermining any proposal with "but" and "if" statements. We had an issue in our group when we wanted to expand membership to 40 people. One of our firebrand partners, Wendell Holden, agreed to the idea and exclaimed, "We definitely need to bring in new partners, but I think we should wait until next year." You should watch out for these types of statements, addressing them immediately, or else trouble is coming.

3. "Confusion"

This is actually the hardest to overcome because a knowledge gap usually exists. We recently structured a complex real estate transaction and it was going to be hard to get group consent without support from our leaders. During one of the meetings, partner Ryan Williams said, "Hold up. I'm confused and I just don't understand where you're coming from." No matter how long it takes, confusion like this has to be addressed and resolved so that everyone has a clear understanding. Sometimes, you'll have to agree on letting those "in the know" make the decision. But, it's critical to have ideas and concepts summarized so everyone can understand. If you can't put the idea on one page, it is not worth talking about. If you can manage these negative reactions, you can create a cohesive collective mentality—ultimately embracing change for the better.

Storing Talent and Maximizing Human Capital

Outside of selling concepts to the group, one other critical component of realizing the storehouse is leveraging everyone's talents. If you don't utilize the greatest resource in an investment group or organization—its people—you will never succeed.

There is an old parable about men with money that will help illustrate this:

A master gave his three servants talents of money. To one he gave five talents of money, to another he gave two talents and to the third he gave one talent, each according to his ability. Then the master left and went on a journey. The man who had received the five talents went at once to put his money to work and gained five more. The servant who had two talents gained two more. The last servant with one talent went off, dug a hole in the ground and hid his master's money.

After a long time, the master of those servants returned to settle his accounts with them. The first and second men had doubled their talents of money and the master rejoiced. "Well done, good and faithful servants!" he said. "You have been faithful with a few things. I will put you in charge of many more. Come and share your master's happiness!"

The man who had received the one talent came and told his master, "I know that you are a demanding man and you have harvested and gathered even when you have not sown or scattered seed. So I was afraid and went out and hid your talent in the ground. See, here is what belongs to you."

His master replied, "You wicked, lazy servant!" He took the talent and gave it to the one who had produced 10, and threw the servant out.

This parable holds significant information on how to leverage skills and manage the group's portfolio. GRIG also utilizes this ideology in its approach to maximizing the organization's human capital.

First, ideas mean nothing without execution. Do not arbitrarily allocate your funds to either certain sectors of stocks or diverse projects. You have to put your money on the people in the organization who can deliver results. This is why GRIG allocates the majority of its time and money to those who have proven themselves worthy of such an investment. This might cause concentration in a certain area, but a focused return on profit is always better than a scattered loss. It also provides insight into personal accountability and responsibility.

Second, don't squander the talents of money, special gifts and skills that you bring to the table. It is the job of leaders to identify and utilize these talents in order to distribute cash accordingly. The master in the parable gave out his money based on skill, and let the individual recipients determine the ultimate use.

Finally, use your people or they will leave. Everyone wants to be a part of something larger than themselves. There is a direct correlation between those who give time and money and the amount of effort they put into the organization.

However, certain people need help in determining how they can participate and add value. The losers will put a drag on the organization by not working and hiding their talents in the ground. It would be in your best interests to let these people go—and quickly. Most winners are either implementing or trying to find a way to do so. It is up to the group to help them in either a small or large way, which will add value to the organization's core storehouse.

The ideas introduced in this chapter really point toward creating a new sense of personal ownership in GRIG, and should produce the same effect in any investment club or organization.

When we call ourselves a family, we really mean it. We look for ways to help each other and make dreams come true for partners. We try to align individuals' goals to GRIG's goals, so that we all benefit. It is a way to live, rather than just a method to invest.

By no means was this an overnight change; we are working every day to maintain this commitment. Many of us were taught to be selfish and to protect what is ours. We still have problems, when new members join, in helping them understand this cultural aspect of the group. Nevertheless, I believe it is one of the reasons for our continued success.

What I Learned
- Teach members how to leverage their talents for the group.

- Understand who are your strongest players and quickly weed out those who provide no benefit or who counter the vision.

- Live the vision of the group—it makes everyone much stronger.

- Don't be fooled by diversification for the sake of diversification; invest in those areas where you are the strongest.

Chapter 8
From Good to Great

Narrated by Marck Dorvil

"Hey gang. How about we make this year's theme 'From Good to Great'?"

It was about 3:00 a. m. I woke up and couldn't go back to sleep. It was one of those times when you just wake up with a lot on your mind. I was thinking about everything, for some reason: my job, my wife and GRIG. Everything was spiraling in my head. I recently made a major career move, leaving my corporate job to join Janelle in real estate. It was a big move for me—one that more than a few of my friends thought was too risky.

Before I left, I was one of the youngest managers at The Home Depot. I had a large budget, a four-man staff and a great deal of responsibility. I reported to a director who in turn

115

reported to the division president. The job was fast paced and high profile. It seemed like the perfect situation—I was young, powerful and making money. I soon realized, however, once I got a taste of the corporate management lifestyle, that it wasn't what I really wanted.

With corporate power comes corporate politics. If you want to continue moving up the ranks, you have to make some hefty personal sacrifices…and heavy sacrifice is what I made to get to that point. Within only one year of joining the company, I was promoted three times, which wasn't an easy accomplishment in such a large company, in so little time. But, I did it through blood, sweat and tears.

I really did not intend to move up as quickly as I did, or to work as hard as I did. I actually left my prior consulting job to work for The Home Depot because I was looking for a better quality of life. You know—less travel, more time at home with my wife. I was still a newlywed, and I hardly saw Janelle. So, I decided to go work in Corporate America, where most consultants go to take a break. But, that's not exactly how it ended up.

The Not So Easy Life

It's kind of funny that most consultants make fun of the clients they work for because they believe that non-consultants don't work as hard, and are simply not as talented. I would say that this is partially true. Some of the consultants I worked with, I could have sworn never slept a wink. It was always work, work and more work. But I wouldn't say that they were always the most productive. There's always a misconception that the harder or longer you work, the more things you get done. The truth is, the smarter and more efficiently you work, the more things you get done.

Take Phillipe, for example. He's a senior manager at PepsiCo and is extremely efficient. He could run circles around many of my former consulting colleagues, who supposedly put in a lot of billable hours.

I came across many competent clients who had managed to get things done in time and leave at a decent hour. I remember that when they would check out at around 5:00, we would crack jokes about them leaving so early, while we burned the midnight oil. We often went to eat and came back to work way into the night, and then came back early the next morning and did it all over again.

I admit that I was one of those consultants who made fun of corporate people. I quietly envied them, though, as they packed up to go home to their wives and children while I got to hang around a few type A personalities who thought a little too much of themselves. Don't get me wrong; they weren't all bad. Some of the folks I worked with were incredibly bright, not to mention humble.

One particular person named Bob, was so genuine that when I eventually left the consulting life, I made sure to bring him along with me. I put him in front of the right people to give him the best shot at getting hired. Bob was so sharp that within a few years of joining the new company, he was promoted to director. He is what Jim Collins, author of *From Good to Great*, would call a "Level 5 leader."

I actually aspired to become a leader like Bob and to develop an organization that had the unique qualities Jim Collins mentioned in his book. Little did I know that I would soon be challenging GRIG to meet the call to greatness.

From Bad to Good (to Bad again?)

As I lay with all of these thoughts in my mind, I thought back to how my dreams of corporate bliss had gone haywire, eventually causing me to leave Corporate America to venture into the entrepreneurial realm. Looking back, it's almost comical how it happened. After deciding to leave consulting, I landed an interview with the internal audit group of The Home Depot. There was a small process improvement arm that piqued my interest. I interviewed for the position and got the job. Easy, right?

I thought I was well on my way to a better work/life balance. Little did I know that the entire audit team was going through reorganization, and I would soon be thrust into a new position in a newly created, high-profile group.

No more than a couple of months after I joined the group, I had to re-interview for my job. The department laid off everyone, and we all had to re-interview for the new positions. The internal audit group was split into two separate groups: traditional audit and a new leadership rotation program. Oh, boy, what had I gotten myself into?

The new round of interviews was much more intense than any I had ever experienced before. The process was separated into three parts: an individual interview, a case study with a panel review and a math and writing exam. I remember thinking that this might be the shortest-lived career I ever had. If I didn't pass this new and much more difficult interview process, I could find myself out of a job...one I had only obtained just a few short months before!

Well, I did what I always do when faced with a challenge. I sized up the situation, prepared as best I could and executed with precision. End result: I was rehired and promoted at the same time. Yes! I did it! Way to go, Marck!

Unfortunately, my relief and happiness was short lived. For after that moment, my work/life balance was turned completely upside down. Just to keep up with the high demands of the job, I would stay late into the night to manage the workload. And I wasn't the only one who worked hard in this high-profile group. It was a long-running joke that there were the same amount of cars parked on weekends as there were on weekdays. I can recall many nights of going home at two in the morning only to come back the next day at six a. m. sharp. And just like that, I was right back where I had started.

Fast forward two years and I was a young finance manager with employees older than me, a big budget and easy access to a division president. What had I sacrificed for all of this? Countless sleepless nights at the job, loss of weight due to poor diet, minimal contact with Janelle and a reduction in my extracurricular activities—including GRIG.

Extracurricular Versus Generational Wealth

I remember a telephone conversation I had with Phillipe and Ryan during this time. As I served as the senior partner, Phillipe was my financial partner and Ryan was my junior partner. I sat back in my chair at my home office and hit the speaker button. Their voices echoed around the room. Looking up at my ceiling, I listened.

"Marck, man, you're running yourself into the ground. Why are you pushing yourself so hard?" asked Ryan.

"I often ask myself the same question, Ryan. I don't know

how to take it slow. Everything I do, I put 110 percent into it. Even if it's killing me."

"Well, Marck," Phillipe said, "I know you have responsibilities at the job, but you also have responsibilities with GRIG. You know you're the senior partner. People look to you for guidance and direction. We'll try to hold down the fort, but we really need you to be involved and engaged. The group needs its leader and at this time, that person happens to be you."

I thought for a second. "I know, Phillipe, but GRIG is becoming more of an extracurricular thing for me right now. I have to focus on my career and paying the bills." There was a moment of silence; actually, a long moment of silence. I kind of got the impression that I had said something taboo. Boy, had I been right about that!

"Extracurricular activity? What the hell is that supposed to mean? Is that how you think of GRIG?" Phillipe blasted back. "I can't believe that after all this time, and all we've done, you still consider GRIG just extracurricular!" I couldn't see him, but I could tell that his face was red hot.

Before the situation got out of hand, Ryan had jumped in with a calm voice. "Listen Marck, we know you have a lot on your plate at work, but so do we. What I think you need to realize is that we're prioritizing a little differently than you. Sure, we can choose to spend countless hours at our jobs, but we choose to spend some of that time on GRIG. Why? We get fulfillment out of it. GRIG is not just a game to us—it's our future livelihood. And although it might not be paying the bills right now, it will someday, not only for us but for future generations."

Ryan continued, "Remember our mission you spear-headed? Remember generational wealth? That's what it's all about. Now, if you need us to take up some slack for you, we will, but it has to be temporary, or it doesn't make sense for you to stay onboard as our leader. For such a high-profile position, we can't afford to have someone who is not fully committed."

His comments really resonated with me. I had been looking at it all wrong. It was at that moment that I realized that, somewhere along the way up the corporate ladder, I had lost the true essence of why I joined GRIG.

I had a choice to make: either get back into the swing of things or relieve myself of my position. I had to look deep into myself to find out what I really wanted in life. Would I choose to make GRIG an integral part of my life or just another extracurricular activity?

GRIG Is a Business, Not a Game
"So, which is it? Are you in or are you out?" Phillipe asked, still seeming a little frustrated. You would think I just tried to hit his kid or something. But what I first translated as anger was really unyielding passion for the survival and continued success of the group. It was almost instinctual in nature the way Phillipe reacted. Almost like a father trying to make sure his baby was going to be okay.

And with a long pause and deafening silence, I said, "I'm in." From that point on, I made sure never to think of GRIG as extracurricular again. Ryan was right: GRIG is not just a game, it's a business.

I refocused and reenergized. I went back to work with the

goal of creating a better balance. I forced myself to be more efficient and didn't care who saw me cutting out early. As long as I had my work done, they couldn't say a thing.

Well, except give me more work, which they did. It's funny, the more successful you are at getting things done, the more work you're given.

I must admit that it was challenging, but I managed it. I also devised an exit strategy that would eventually allow me and my wife to go into business together and ultimately create a stronger relationship with GRIG.

I successfully branched out to become a full-time Realtor with Janelle. She actually left her corporate job a year before me to build up the business. By the time I was ready to get out; she had already created a strong clientele. I, of course, came in and set policies and procedures to improve our operating efficiencies. A few years later, we partnered with GRIG to open up our own full-service real estate company, ERA Executive Realty in Atlanta GA. It's been a blast ever since.

Making this move was tough at first, but it paid off big. From a relationship standpoint between me, my wife and GRIG, I developed an overall better quality of life. Once I renewed my dedication to GRIG, I was laser focused. At that point in my tenure, I wanted to become more strategic while maintaining a keen eye on operations. I wanted to think more long-range, while accounting for short-term results. And I wanted the entire management team to be on the same page.

I thought about my friend Bob and his leadership style, and I thought about our investment group and where I could take it. I thought about the talented people in the group and their passion to keep growing. At that point, I realized that I had a new motto to champion, one that would again take us to a whole new level: "From Good to Great."

Achieving Greatness

The annual meeting theme is very important, for it sets the tone and gives everyone a vision of what's to come. At our first planning session, my recommendation to make the theme of the upcoming annual meeting "From Good to Great" was greeted with silence.

"I think it would be fitting," I explained, "since we are really trying to separate ourselves from just another good investment group."

Jennesia broke the silence. "I like it. I think it's very fitting for what we are trying to do." She was one of those people who didn't say very much, but when she did, everyone listened. Although we had a few female team leads, Jennesia was the only female manager in the group at the time, and she held her own. She was our recording partner and a damned good one, too. I made sure she was on my management team because I wanted a woman's point of view and someone who was not scared of cooling down some of the male testosterone. She took advantage of her position, and extended her responsibilities and influence like any good manager would do.

An attorney by trade, she would later become our parliamentarian and newly created general counsel, where she would head up our team of other attorneys in the group. I've always made it a point to get her opinion on just about anything I have an idea about. Usually, it's just calling her to get feedback or level set my ideas. I have to admit that several times, I've called to get her thoughts before I talked to Ryan or Phillipe.

Sometimes, my ideas never passed her ears. If she thought it was a bad idea, she wouldn't be shy about telling me. But at this point, I hadn't talked to anyone about the theme. So, when she gave me her stamp of approval, I was pleased.

"Thanks, Jennesia. It comes from a book I read a while back by Jim Collins. There are a lot of teachings in that book I think we can model ourselves after. But I'm open to hearing other suggestions, and we can vote on the best ones." A few other people keyed in and said that they liked the theme. A few more suggestions were also thrown on the table, and we voted. It was unanimous: "From Good to Great" would be our next annual meeting theme.

Long-term Roadmap

Like any goal, you need a plan for delivery and completion. Going from good to great would be no easy feat. One thing we do well is planning from year to year, and executing our team objectives. Between creating objectives, allocating resources, setting approval authorities and a host of other activities, we work like a well-oiled machine. The challenge was to think longer term than just one year, to connect the dots over multiple years and to determine where we would be a few years out.

That type of planning took some considerable work and creativity. We tried to do this in prior years, but it had not proven successful. I think the key reason it did not succeed is because we lacked the proper strategic planning tools.

Years ago, when I was a consultant, we developed something called a "strategic roadmap" for a large, international chemical company. The roadmap had essentially laid out the company's strategy in phases, with each successive phase taking the company to a higher level. This tool had allowed the company to identify all of the objectives it needed to achieve in order to be at a certain place within a certain timeframe.

Armed with this tool, I devised a strategic planning session with the GRIG managers. We talked about all of the things we thought were possible in our future and what needed to happen for us to get there. I facilitated the discussions as key managers weighed in.

Phillipe actually came up with a great improvement to the model. He suggested that after we come up with all of the objectives for each phase, we should go back and identify our big bets—the things that were most critical to our success.

The other objectives were important, but these big bets were absolutely necessary for our growth as an organization. We spent countless hours working on the roadmap and finalizing all the minute details.

I remember looking at the finished product probably as Leonardo da Vinci did after painting the Mona Lisa. It was remarkable what this group could do when we focused and put our minds together. At our best, we could do anything. We decided to present the final results at our appropriately titled "From Good to Great" annual meeting.

The Birth of GRIGFS

Around the same time as the meeting, we were introduced to an individual who wanted to partner with GRIG to promote his products and services.

We toyed with this concept in the past, but had never put any real weight on it. It's amazing how many good ideas cross your path but never see the light of day simply because you did not put in the required effort to see them to fruition.

Providing products and services to individuals outside of GRIG was both alluring and intimidating. How would we organize ourselves to meet this need? Could this be part of our long-term strategic plan?

One thing we knew for sure was that this would fundamentally change the way GRIG would see itself moving forward.

We always focused on internal partners and were comfortable with doing just that. Now, we were introducing ourselves to a whole new world, one that could provide us the most financial benefits yet. I remember receiving the call from Phillipe, when he recommended that we create a brand new entity called GRIGFS. This would be a new group, run by a president, with the sole purpose of identifying and selling products and services to the external market. Hence, the birth of GRIG Financial Services—or GRIGFS.

Phillipe was so excited when he called me, it became contagious. "This is huge, Marck. This new entity will revolutionize GRIG's go-to-market strategy! The amount of money to be made is limitless! We know there's a need for products and services we can provide. We've been very successful helping ourselves. This is a natural transition to help others build wealth and build more wealth for us in the process!"

His excitement was like a shot of adrenaline. Although he was on the other side of the phone, I felt like he was right next to me. The vision of this paradigm shift swept through me and I finally exclaimed, "I believe!"

As a result of many conversations, we came up with a range of solid ideas that GRIGFS should entertain, such as forming a strategic alliance with another reputable organization, creating an external investment marketplace and developing a small-business consulting model. Of course, all of these required some due diligence, and a placement in our strategic roadmap.

I then talked with Phillipe about resources.

"Well, it has to be someone the group trusts, someone who is a leader and who has built strong credibility in the organization over a long period of time."

At that moment, we both shouted, "Ryan!" He was a good fit for the role for many reasons. At the time, he was second in command as junior partner, and in this role, he demonstrated time and again that he was more than capable of getting things done. I was thinking of finishing out my term as senior partner in order for Ryan to step up. But, this seemed like a better opportunity for him to really take something from scratch and grow it.

I called Ryan to break the news with hopefully the same level of excitement Phillipe had when he'd mentioned it to me.

"Hmm, so I would be president of a new entity? What would that entail?" Ryan always thought through the minutest detail before agreeing to or signing up for anything.

"It would be a subsidiary of GRIG. We would provide you with all the resources to get it off the ground. The goal would be for you to eventually develop your own group to complete your objectives."

"Sounds like a lot of work. Do we have the resources?"

"Well, what do you think you would need, Ryan?"

He sighed deeply and said, "For something like this, I think I need a full-time resource."

Wow, a full-time resource working for GRIG. The thought sent chills down my spine. Up until that point, I always thought of us as a strictly volunteer organization. Having a full-time resource would change all of that—hopefully, for the better.

"It won't be easy, but I think we might be able to manage that request."

History in the Making!
I called an emergency management meeting to align all of the leaders in the group. With help from Phillipe and Ryan, I discussed this new vision and what it would take to make it happen. After a brief discussion, everyone was onboard. We then went to work, and set up a detailed job profile and a full set of interview questions. We solicited the group for candidates and started interviewing. We thought it was important to

hire someone whom the partners already knew and who could hit the ground running because of his or her understanding of our internal processes.

After a lengthy process, Harvey, the junior financial partner at the time, made history when he accepted the full-time position with GRIGFS. He was formally given the position and the announcement was made to the group. It was important to establish up front the high business standards we expected from our first full-time resource. If successful, Harvey would be the first of many full-time hires working for GRIG.

After working out a few details, we added GRIGFS to our roadmap. Now, it was time to put a good team together. Starting at the top, Ryan knew he needed a good second in command. That was where Malcolm, the former ventures team lead, came in. Malcolm would be instrumental in developing the overall strategy of the new entity. With a background in SBA loans, he knew what it took to get a new small business up and running. Phillipe volunteered to help the group in its initial growth stage, acting more like a consultant when help was needed.

Ryan also needed an executioner. That was where Vianka, lead of the communications team, came in. Of all the GRIG members, I think Vianka and I are most alike. It's kind of scary when I think of it, but we are so in tune, we can usually finish each other's thoughts. I joke that Vianka is my second wife. It's a long-running joke that I made sure to let my wife in on. With an exotic name like Vianka Perez Belyea, I have to make sure Janelle knows that there's no funny business going on between us. But all kidding aside, Vianka is the consummate project manager. She can take any situation and make sure that the end results are better than you could ever expect.

Over the years, my trust and admiration for Vianka have continued to grow. I knew her expertise would be tested to its limits with this high-impact, high-visibility group. But I knew she could handle it. Bringing Vianka onboard also allowed Ryan to focus on the big picture, and have faith that at the operational-level things were being done.

It's Time Our Story Is Told
It was around this time that several people were expressing interest in joining GRIG due to the article published in *Black Enterprise*, praising our group as one of the top investment clubs in the country. We were inundated with calls and emails asking how we got to where we were. Ryan took a genuine interest in these comments and requests, and suggested we develop a toolkit to sell to people interested in not only creating but maintaining successful investment groups.

I thought it was a brilliant idea that could be added to the GRIGFS initiatives. But I challenged him to take it one step further. "Why not create a book?" I asked. The book would not only tell our story, but provide the valuable steps, tools and "how-to"s for creating and successfully running an investment group. He agreed.

Thus, another chapter in GRIG's history was created. This time, it would be for the entire world to read.

What I Learned
• Develop a long-term strategy and break it down into manageable phases.

• Focus on the "big bets" that will propel your group forward.

• Look outside your group for creative methods of attracting new dollars to the group.

• When you are ready, bring on a full-time resource to take you to the next level.

• Tell others your story, so that they may be able to profit as you have.

Conclusion

Narrated by Phillipe Tatem

To think it was more than 10 years ago when the idea of GRIG was born among college students. At the time, we had a bright idea, but no idea of how far we could grow. Now, those same college students are today's entrepreneurs, managers in Corporate America, lawyers, business owners—you name it; more than 40 GRIG members from across the globe. As we look back, we are amazed at what we have accomplished and we look forward to much more.

When we first began this book, we wanted to answer the question, "How did we do it?" We also wanted to provide guidance for how you too can do it. All the years of dedication, passion and commitment are provided to you in this book to learn from and prosper.

Throughout this journey, we encountered a lot of bumps, bruises and curve balls. But as we struggled, we learned. And as we persevered, we became stronger. There were times when we were sure that the group would fall apart. We not only survived, we thrived!

From this book, we hope you have gained the know-how to grow your own money tree through building a strong investment group. By planting the seed of collective economics, you can achieve financial empowerment and escape the path most of our parents had to walk. Maybe you have even attained the power to influence others, to learn from others and to manage others.

Outside of what you can learn from us, you already have a lot of knowledge. You have always known how to be part of a group or team. Remember when you played football, sung in the choir or even worked on a group project for class? Why not seek financial reward with a group, where everyone plays a part to make a championship team, or the next group of millionaires next door?

We are often taught in the incorrect teachings of success and how to gain it. It is really not an individual sport and working together can finally get you to higher levels. No longer should you be limited by statements like, "Money doesn't grow on trees!" This is where imagination is killed and dreamers are crushed.

The real secret is that while individuals may achieve a level of financial, educational and networking success, your potential is unlimited when you work as a group. As you grow in your financial empowerment, consider your next steps, such as creating your own investment group or joining an existing investment group—maybe even GRIG!

Learn from our stories; let our experiences serve as guideposts for you. Use our lessons and strategies for managing the good and bad times. Good luck on your journey and see you at the top!

Become part of our network and join the story at www. grig. com.

Helpful Definitions

• Annual meeting: a meeting that official bodies and associations are often required by law (or by the constitution or charter governing the body) to hold. The annual meeting is held every year to inform the group's members of previous and future activities. It is generally the forum for the election of officers or directors for the organization. It is also an opportunity for the shareholders and partners to receive copies of the company's accounts and review fiscal information, as well as ask any questions regarding the decisions the business will take in the future.

• Asset allocation: the strategy of diversifying your portfolio into different investment classes.

• Buying on margin: borrowing up to half of the purchase price of a security from your broker.

• Collective economics: the principle of collective economics expounds the value of individuals pooling money to invest in larger opportunities to create wealth.

• Dow Jones Industrial Average (DJIA): sometimes referred to as "the Dow," it is the most widely known and reported market indicator.

• Economic rights movement: provides a new mindset as it pertains to money issues we face today, and develops actions to improve the economic profile.

• Human capital: refers to the stock or resource of productive skills and technical knowledge embodied in labor.

• Initial public offering (IPO): the first sale of a corporation's common shares to investors on a public stock exchange. The main purpose of an IPO is to raise capital for the corporation.

• Investment group/club: a group of people who pool their money to make investments. Usually, investment clubs are organized as partnerships and, after the members study different investments, the group decides to buy or sell based on a majority vote of the members. Club meetings may be educational and each member may actively participate in investment decisions.

• Investment strategy: an investor's plan of distributing assets among various investments, taking into consideration such factors as individual goals, risk tolerance and horizon.

• Limited liability company (LLC): in the law of many of the United States, this is a legal form of business offering limited liability to its owners. It is similar to a corporation but is often a more flexible form of ownership, especially suitable for smaller companies with a limited number of owners. Unlike a regular corporation, a limited liability company with one member may be treated as a disregarded entity, so the member is often singled out as a person performing the actions of the LLC. A limited liability company with multiple members may choose, generally at the time that the new entity applies for a US federal taxpayer ID number, to be treated for US federal taxation purposes as a partnership, as a C corporation or as an S corporation. An LLC can elect to be either member managed or manager managed.

• Margin account: an account that you hold with a broker where you can borrow up to 50 percent of a stock's price and buy with the combined funds of your money and the borrowed money.

• NASDAQ: one of three major US stock markets. Unlike traditional exchanges, it has no central trading location and no exchange floor. Rather, it is an advanced telecommunications and computer network, run by the National Association of Securities Dealers, that allows brokers to monitor stock prices, match orders and make trades from anywhere in the country.

• Operating agreement: an agreement that specifies the rights and duties of the members of a group; how the group will be managed; what number of votes is required for a particular action; who gets what share of the profits and losses of the group; what to do in the case of a dispute; when, how and for what price a member can sell his ownership of the group; when and how the group can be dissolved; and the like.

• Price earnings (P/E) ratio: shows the relationship between a stock's price and the company's earnings for the last four quarters. It's figured by dividing the current price per share by the earnings per share.

• Request for information (RFI): a standard business process, the purpose of which is to collect written information about the capabilities of various suppliers. Normally, it follows a format that can be used for comparative purposes.

• SMART objectives: SMART is a mnemonic used in project management at the project objective-setting stage. It is a way of evaluating if the objectives that are being set are appropriate for the individual project. A SMART objective is one that is specific, measurable, achievable, relevant and time framed.

• Strategic roadmap: a planning tool that enables management to lay out a company's long term strategy in phases, with each successive phase taking the company to a higher level.

• SWOT analysis: a strategic planning tool used to evaluate the strengths, weaknesses, opportunities and threats involved in a project or business venture. It involves specifying the objective of the business venture or project and identifying the internal and external factors that are favorable and unfavorable to achieving that objective.

• Tulip mania: the term is used metaphorically to refer to any large economic bubble. It originally came from a period in the history of the Netherlands, during which demand for tulip bulbs reached such a peak that enormous prices were charged for a single bulb. It took place in the first part of the 17th century.

For tools and templates discussed in this book, please visit us online.